The
Healing is Mutual:

Marriage Empowerment Tools™ to Rebuild
Trust and Respect—Together

The
Healing is Mutual:

Marriage Empowerment Tools™ to Rebuild Trust and Respect—Together

Deb Schwarz Hirschhorn, Ph.D.

Mill City Press

Mill City Press, Inc.
212 3rd Avenue North, Suite 290
Minneapolis, MN 55401
612.455.2294
www.millcitypublishing.com

ISBN-13: 978-1-937600-78-5
LCCN: 2012931606

Printed in the United States of America

Dedication

This book is dedicated to my family who believes in me and to my clients who teach me. Thank you, Daddy, for the unflagging encouragement you used to give me. I have not seen you in over thirty years, but your love, your kindness, your values, your spirituality, your warmth are strong in my life. You have been a presence even though you are not with us. Thank you, Mom, for giving me life at great sacrifice. Thank you for caring and trying.

To my present family, the family that you and I created, Matt, what can I say? I am blown away by God's goodness. Thank you, Matt, for supporting me and pushing me to follow my dreams. To Chana Leah, I am awed by your incisive mind; your advice, probing questions, and suggestions were pivotal in making this book happen. To Tevi, who is more than web designer and user experience analyst, but a powerful creative force, thank you. To Yedidya and Btzalel, your love and cheerleading has meant more to me than you can know.

To Harlan Kilstein who first encouraged me to put my ideas into a book, thank you.

To my mother-in-law, Sadie, thank you again and again for your support and your smile.

To my many clients who have honored me by sharing their most private stories—along with their suffering—thank you for teaching me the meaning of courage and human frailty. Thank you for asking the hard questions and being brave enough to listen to some answers.

Thank you, too, to Barbara Fischkin who asked great questions and caught all the mistakes no one else did and to the cheerful people at Mill City Press who endured my endless questions and gently propelled me forward.

Introduction

The Healing is Mutual addresses the most serious problems in marriage such as broken communication, verbal and emotional abuse, neglect, and infidelity. It was written to help both partners heal—and that includes the hurtful partner.

That means you won't find finger-pointing here—even at people who behave badly. If they learn to use even a few of the tools in this book, the meanness will disappear.

You will get the most out of this book if you both read it together. There are a number of self-help marriage books out there for just one partner to read and work on alone. Unfortunately, those books are not geared to turn around the hurtful person. That's because the one who is doing the hurting is afraid to read the book!

The way those books work is by showing the wounded partner how to avoid getting sucked into arguments with the other partner. That is good advice, but it leaves the offended partner *alone* trying to turn things around. And it leaves the unkind partner without tools to be better.

If you're hurt, I don't want you to be left alone while your partner remains unkind.

Instead, leave this book or a useful page on the kitchen table for your partner to find so that the two of you can work on it together. I'd like to help you really be partners again.

While you heal, I'd like you to be my partner in helping your partner to heal, too. You see, *people who act mean have been hurt themselves.* And until they heal inside, they aren't able to control their tempers, and be compassionate, considerate, and respectful. So, please gently encourage your partner to use the tools and give ample credit when you see him or her using them. When you do that, you will promote healing as much as the tools in this book do.

That's why the central point of this book is healing for both spouses. The idea here is that *if each person heals, the marriage heals. If one person remains unhealed, both people will suffer.*

Research supports that even verbal abusers can change. [1,2,3,4] That change will not take place in an atmosphere of confrontation and blame. It will take place through self-reflection, self-nurturing, self-understanding, self-discipline, and skill-building. This process begins with recognition that feelings are being bruised in this relationship. Many therapists have missed this. Initially, the problem was so bad that when couples would come to therapists for marriage counseling, thousands of cases of *physical* violence would go undetected. [5,6,7,8] If they missed physical violence, they surely missed mental cruelty, especially since the latter can be so subtle.

You might think that women's rights advocates who do understand domestic violence would not miss the cues. They, therefore, would probably not miss emotional mistreatment, either. Although they would not miss domestic violence, handling it safely is equally important. If women's rights advocates don't handle domestic violence cases correctly, we cannot rely on them to have answers in cases of mental cruelty.

It is standard practice for domestic violence advocates to advise victims to leave the relationship. However, research shows that leaving is *more dangerous* than staying at the time of leaving and for two years afterwards. [9,10,11,12] That is because the angry person is inflamed even more by a partner leaving.

Thus, focusing on healing violent people is quite pragmatic: It ensures the safety of victims.

Now you might be wondering, "But DrDeb, what has violence to do with me?"

Introduction

I have three answers for that.

First, you'd be surprised what violence really is. Did you know that if one person blocks a doorway during an argument, that's considered violent? You will see why as we go forward. So you might actually be in a violent relationship after all.

Second, emotional and verbal aggression escalates. It can end up physical. Therefore, detection of emotional aggression is imperative to prevent physical aggression.

Third, the right time to leave a relationship is not when it is emotionally destructive. That's bad timing. It means intolerable levels of toxicity will be injected into the divorce process. If you must divorce, learn to get along first so you avoid a "messy" one.

I am awed and impressed by the many people who do decide to stay and see that they and their partners get the healing they need. Here are some of their reasons:

- They believe in marriage and want to make it work.
- They believe that their partner is a good person in spite of awful behavior.
- They attribute their partner's bad behavior to childhood suffering and believe that addressing the past will change the present behavior.
- They have children who love both parents and they want to keep their family intact.
- They recognize that divorce will not provide a cure for the other person's damaging behavior.
- They would rather work things out than see their net worth dwindle down to nothing in a costly divorce.

There's more. This book isn't just about eliminating verbal pain. It's also about couples who don't quarrel at all because they have nothing to say to one another, leaving each person feeling alone in the marriage. Some of these people ease their pain by cheating. This book is also for these couples.

To get the most out of this book, both partners should try out all of the tools, either separately or together. But if you only take away a few, that's a good start.

Take it slow. Read and digest. Don't rush it.

Because I want to help you as you go forward, I have two additional tools for you. If you go to www.TheHealingIsMutual.com/download, you will find an audio file and a text file from me. The audio file is a relaxation which I created. You will see more about how that plays into your healing as you read further. The text is a cheat-sheet that I created to help people be assertive. It is also a sneak preview of my forthcoming assertiveness book. Many of my clients have found this one-page review of assertive tools to be invaluable.

Note that both men and women are victims; both are abusers, too. The book interchanges "he" and "she" randomly.

Part I introduces a core idea of this book: victim thinking, how to pinpoint it and how to put brakes on it.

Part II examines emotional and verbal mistreatment, how to stop doing it, how to get your needs met without it, and how to heal from it.

Part III assumes you have now gotten past the cruelty and pain described in Part II and presents further ways for each of you to heal individually.

Part IV takes healing to the next level; it is about healing the relationship, and turning your marriage into a source of healing for the pain with which you came into it. It is about building true intimacy and real love.

Introduction

The tools in this book address your thoughts, your behavior, your feelings, and your soul. All of these are part of you. Therefore, no matter what your preferred learning style, there's something here for you. My goal is for these strategies to empower you to heal from old wounds while you rebuild trust and respect together.

Table Of Contents

Part I   A Peek Behind the Closed Door

Chapter One	Will the Real Victim Please Stand Up?	1
Chapter Two	You Want to *Heal* Ricky, too?	23

Part II   How We Hurt Each Other – And How We Heal

Chapter Three	Do You *Really* Know What Violence Is?	29
Chapter Four	Power and Voice	41
Chapter Five	Name-Calling Is No Big Deal—Or Is It?	57
Chapter Six	"My Partner is Hypersensitive"	71
Chapter Seven	Put-downs: They're No Joke	83
Chapter Eight	Blame Boomerangs	93
Chapter Nine	Body Language Roars	119
Chapter Ten	Scaring into Submission	125
Chapter Eleven	Rejecting, Neglecting, and Cheating	139
Chapter Twelve	Build Barriers to Backsliding	149
Chapter Thirteen	Six Things to Keep in Mind	169

Part III   Empowering Yourself

Chapter Fourteen	Eight Healing Activities for Your "Self"	179
Chapter Fifteen	Laughing Is Better than Crying	195
Chapter Sixteen	Increase Your Sensitivity	201

Part IV: Rebuilding Your Marriage

Chapter Seventeen	Sixteen Things to Do to Reconcile —and Ignite that Spark!	213
Chapter Eighteen	The *Real* Law of Attraction: Opposites or Likes?	253

Endnotes	261
Bibliography	269

PART I

A PEEK BEHIND THE CLOSED DOOR:

RICKY AND JEAN

Don't be surprised if Ricky and Jean resemble you and your partner in some ways. Part I introduces them. We will be following them—and Wanda; Bernie and Melanie; Smitty and Rachael; Betty; Sydney and Arthur; Manny and Sylvia; Ed and Cheryl; Lillian and Matthew; Shaindy and Yossi; Harry, Marcia's boss and her husband, Steve; and many other people—throughout this book.

Chapter One
Will the Real Victim Please Stand Up

Jean hesitantly picks up the phone. She's never done this before. This feels so weird. But then again, weird is much better than the awful feeling she has been having that her marriage is falling apart. Yes, weird is definitely the lesser of two evils, so she dials. She thinks about the last fight they had. Her husband, Ricky had raised his voice, and it was terrible. And that was at the end of a long litany of mistreatment.

Jean calls a marriage counselor and tells her about being yelled at. The conversation with the therapist turns out not so bad. The therapist seems nice, friendly, human, and Jean feels comfortable making the appointment.

At the meeting, the therapist has Jean and Ricky fill out some paperwork, and then she proceeds to ask how all the problems started. Jean, who really never understood why her husband has treated her so badly, wants to hear his side as much as the therapist does, so she asks him to go first.

"You wanna know the truth?" Ricky replies. "It started last Thursday. I come home from work. I work hard. I come home and—I can't believe it—my wife and her sister are in MY living room painting it baby blue. I was shocked. I felt like she had punched me in the gut. Painting not the baby's room, not a little study, but our living room. Without any discussion whatsoever! Baby blue! That's not right. Would you say that's right?" he challenges the counselor.

"No," the therapist answers, "that doesn't seem right to just go ahead without discussion."

"And that's how it always is. I'm nobody in my own home. Just a nothing." He spits the words out and smacks one hand into the palm of the other. "That wasn't the first time, either. My wife, Jean, she had people over for dinner last week, and I came home all tired and ready to flop on the couch

1

and there they were, for Pete's sake."

Let's hit the "pause" button here for a minute and take a look at this. You know and I know and Ricky knows in his heart of hearts that nothing his wife has done deserves for him to yell at her—even if her behavior was wrong. But he thinks he is a victim. He feels like a victim, like the outsider in his own marriage.

Does this sound familiar? Whether or not it is true, it is Ricky's perception that he is a victim. From his perspective, she started by leaving him out. And the reason he did what he did is *not* because he wanted to control her but because he felt powerless. He is clueless about how to be noticed, how to be a part of the family, how to get basic respect. Clueless. When, from his perspective, he has taken enough guff, he lashes out.

However, the steam took a few days to build up. The painting project occurred on a Thursday. The fight took place in the wee hours of the morning Saturday.

"So what happened next?" the therapist wanted to know.

"I just went to my room," Ricky replied.

"And sulked?" the therapist gently challenged.

"Yeah," he admitted. "What else was there to do? The paint was paid for; the women were working; I was left out. I didn't talk to her pretty much that night. She didn't seem to want to talk to me, either. The next day, I got up early for work and got out of the house before we had a chance to get into an argument."

Let's hit "pause" again. This part of the story demonstrates what I said above: This man had no idea how to proceed. All he knew how to do was to lick his wounds. He thought: "It is pointless to discuss anything with her because we'll only argue." But look how far away they have drifted as a couple. And the farther away they are, the harder it will be to come back—and the more likely to take a wrong turn.

Returning to the story . . .

Ricky continued, "So when I got home Friday evening, we had dinner plans with her sister and her husband, Neil. It was our only outing since the baby came. A lady where Jean works volunteered to babysit this one time. Now, Neil and I get along. He's a good guy. So, with the four of us out, I started to unwind. One thing led to another, and we started to kid around with our waitress. You know how it is," he said.

"No," said the therapist, who knows never to make assumptions. "What do you mean?"

Ricky became uncomfortable here, but with persistence, the therapist got out of him that he remarked to Neil, regarding the waitress, "Look at her butt, nice and tight." And, of course, he laughed with all his heart.

Let's "pause" here again. Ricky's behavior is awful. He is typical of individuals who don't know how to handle what they perceive as mistreatment. As he dished it back, he felt a sense of release and the stress left him. He was not thinking of Jean's feelings—or those of the innocent waitress—only his own. He was feeling on the losing end of the battle of the sexes; he was feeling like he'd been dumped on, and all he was trying to do was create a fair playing field.

Needless to say, Jean was wounded beyond words. She rushed out of the dining area to the ladies' room, crying. Ricky felt a hollow feeling form in the pit of his stomach. Now he'd really get it, he thought. She composed herself and returned to the table, eating the rest of her meal in stony silence. The men tried to kid around to lighten the mood, but it didn't work. Eventually they all left—and the fireworks started when they got home. Jean's dignity had been so badly wounded that she felt she had to level a verbal attack at Ricky. Ricky felt justified because of his own hurt,

3

so he countered verbally. And then, as is the case all too frequently, the argument escalated to rage, late into the night.

"Can you tell me," the therapist questioned, "whether there has ever been violence?"

"Actually," Ricky answered, "the answer is 'never,' although, honestly, I've felt close to it at times."

Now, the counselor wanted to know what happened from Jean's perspective. Ricky now had the opportunity to hear Jean's side.

The counselor's first question was, "Can you think back as far as necessary to how this whole mess started?" Jean looked tired, worn.

"Yes," she replied softly, "we've had problems since the beginning. Well, not the very beginning. No." Her voice trailed off as she reconnected with old memories. "We were very much in love in the beginning." Jean took a deep breath. "He was handsome and dashing. He would do anything for me. He was funny and wonderful. It seemed as if nothing could go wrong if he was there.

"But after the baby came six months ago, I was tired and he always wanted sex. It seemed like he didn't believe me when I said I was tired. He started getting angry at me. It really hurt my feelings. Meanwhile, I didn't feel like I had anyone to lean on, except my sister. I was so tired. You know, I work full time, too. And I had to do all the housework and take care of Goldie, our baby. He didn't lift a finger. Well, I'm used to that," she concluded. "I've been on my own since I was sixteen."

"Why do you suppose he got angry?" the therapist interjected.

"I don't know. He's selfish, I guess," Jean answered.

Let's "pause" again. When one person feels targeted, it is nearly always impossible for that person to see the other person's point of view. This is a case in point. Back when the baby came, Jean had not yet been mistreated. However, Ricky's failure to help certainly made her feel close to it.

Her husband was definitely confused about women. He did not understand the basic biology accompanying motherhood. He did not understand that after a baby, it is nearly *impossible* for a woman to want sex. Her body just isn't ready. Although having a baby is a natural thing, giving birth is akin to doing an Olympics run while being pounded. And then comes the actual childcare: the night feedings, the nursing, the constant burping and changing. And on top of that, there is the regular house care, and Jean had to go back to work. There is *no* humanly possible way to do that without feeling plenty tired. Sex would be the last thing on her mind.

If Jean felt taken advantage of, Ricky also felt like he was on the short end of the stick. Here's this tiny little baby intruding into his life, and he can't get any attention. There is a part of him that knows he is being silly; after all, his wife did just go through labor, delivery, and weeks of night feedings. But when will it end?

"Maybe," Ricky thought, "she used her tiredness as an excuse to avoid me."

This is classic *victim thinking*.

Victim Thinking: a Cornerstone of the Mistreatment of Others

People who feel victimized were, indeed, mistreated as children. That's how victim thinking starts: Having been mistreated in childhood, it's only natural to expect to be mistreated again. Therefore, when something feels uncomfortable, victim thinkers jump to the conclusion that the other person intended to be hurtful.

Another element necessary for victim thinking is a lack of outside information. When Ricky was a child, if he'd had a good relationship with a grandma, a clergyperson, a teacher, an after-school counselor, or someone who gave him honest, positive feedback about himself as a human being, then, even though he may have been mistreated at home, the mistreatment would have been countered, and its effects would have been diluted. He might have thought, "I know what my strengths are," and built on them. Then, he would have had solid self-esteem. Apparently, there was no one in Ricky's early life who held up a mirror of his strengths for him to build on.

An example comes from the therapy dialogue with Ricky, as we will see later. He thinks that women are liars. Why? Because, as a child, his father walked out and his mother shuffled him onto other family members, proclaiming that she was "busy," and Ricky didn't believe that. But there's more. There's the unsaid piece, the piece he didn't realize consciously: Women don't lie to *everybody*, just to *him*. What does that imply? It implies that he is not worthy of better treatment. That is the basis of his victim thinking. Victim thinkers don't think they are good enough.

In fact, when I was doing research, that very statement—I wasn't good enough—was the most repeated statement by nearly all of my research subjects. That is the basis upon which each person's self-image is built who becomes an offender or a target of venom. There are other self-deprecating thoughts a person with low self-esteem may have, such as "I am stupid," "I have no future," etc.

Even intelligent, highly competent, successful people can fall into this trap. People who normally know that they are competent and successful can get triggered into the "poor me" mode by circumstances (like being left out of choosing the color of paint, not getting sex anymore, etc.). They know they are good at what they do; nevertheless, even they may not believe in themselves when it comes to relationships.

To sum up, victim thinking happens when:
➤ A person was mistreated as a child

6

- ➤ The mistreated child begins to think poorly of himself
- ➤ There is no outside information refuting her damaging self-thoughts
- ➤ Something happens which triggers these old feelings of being victimized

And now, your healing begins. Let's begin to clear the toxicity of victim thinking out of your head.

(Tool 1) How to Overcome Victim Thinking
Reflect on This . . .
Write your autobiography. Describe the details of your childhood, including the things that hurt you. This is not about blaming your parents. This is about getting clear on how you came to see yourself. What messages did you take away from those experiences? Do you see seeds of victim thinking coming from your childhood?

Before we get too deeply into identifying victim thinking and learning how to overcome it, I'd like to say something *positive* about it. While it is a sad thing for a child to develop an identity of victimhood, it is better than no identity. There are times when, because of mistreatment, children fail to develop a sense of self at all, and that is much worse.

That's how coping skills develop: They're the best small children can do with limited resources and thank God they have them. We should never look down on them. We should, however, recognize when it's time to learn new ones.

Returning to our scenario, the counselor asked Jean what, exactly, was the reason she decided to paint the living room without consulting Ricky. Jean broke down in tears.

"Don't you think I tried?" she wailed. "When he gets into one of his moods, I can't talk to him. I can't think of how many times I tried to bring up the subject over the last few weeks. But he was watching the game, or he had to go out, or he was home late, or our daughter needed someone's attention. And I couldn't stand it. I was depressed enough with everything, and I just absolutely needed a lift. I thought a nice, bright, cheerful color on the wall would pick everyone's spirits up."

There, you have it. The "terrible" thing that the other party did is, ninety-nine times out of one hundred, pretty innocent. Yes, she should have tried harder, but remember, she felt like the butt of his attacks because he got moody, didn't help with housework, and only wanted sex. Yes, he should have tried to talk to her all those times, but he felt like the one at the bottom of the ladder because he thought she was ignoring him the rest of the time.

So who is the REAL victim? Well, they all are. Ricky's mother should have told him, "Sweetie, it's not you." Ricky's father, ditto. By not doing that, they wounded him and taught him to interpret things in a dark way; they taught him to think like a victim. When Jean painted the room without consulting him, she fed into his victim identity.

Jean was damaged too, big time. Innocently trying to be a good mother and wife, she got slammed.

And that poor baby. How will that baby grow up learning to distinguish innocent comments from nasty ones when feelings get injured all too easily? How will she learn to take care of herself with a mother who sets the example of a woman who gets mistreated? How will she learn to relate to her dad when he retreats into his shell? How will she learn to like men with an example like that? How will she come to like *herself* with everybody too busy licking their own wounds to validate her as a person? How is her parents' focus on their own pain any different than the way her paternal grandparents treated her father? How will the cycle of passing down victim thinking to the next generation get broken?

On the other hand, Goldie has not yet become a victim and maybe if Jean and Ricky can master the tools in this book, she never will be. And for all his childhood pain, Ricky is not Jean's victim. He's a victim of his own thinking.

Healing begins with taking an honest look at yourself, including how you see the world.

(Tool 2) How to Overcome Victim Thinking
Reflect on This . . .

Victim thinking can be defined as turning an innocent situation into one in which you decide that someone purposely is trying to hurt you when that is not the case. Have you ever felt that way? Can you recall incidents like that? Take one or two situations in which you *thought* you were mistreated and search for other explanations of what happened.

Playing victim followed by attacking could be called "The Weakness/ Aggressiveness Syndrome" because the aggression comes from a feeling of perceived weakness—being in the "down" position—in the relationship. Ricky was mean in the restaurant to balance out his sense of being unable to somehow right the wrong that he felt was done to him.

Therefore, feeling like the weak one in your relationship may be a clue for you that you have fallen into victim thinking.

Red flags that help you identify victim thinking are crucial to tackling it.

(Tool 3) How to Overcome Victim Thinking
Reflect on This . . .

Do you feel like the weaker person in your relationship? Do you become verbally aggressive as a consequence? Or do you stuff it and sulk? Give examples.

It is just as important, however, to know when you're *not* just thinking like a victim, but in fact, you are one. You may have had a childhood history of trauma as described in Tool 1. You may feel weak in your relationship because you really are, both physically and emotionally.

The chart below is a start in clarifying the differences between actually being victimized and having victim thinking. Use it to start getting clear as to which is the case in your situation. You see, each situation is different. Today you could be actually mistreated as a victim and tomorrow, perhaps you're just thinking like one. Knowing exactly what is happening will help you choose the correct tools to handle it.

Being a Victim vs. Playing Victim

	Current victimization	**Playing** victim
How did it start?	Present mistreatment	Childhood mistreatment
Is the mistreatment continuing?	Yes	No
Are you aware of what is going on?	Maybe, maybe not	Not at all
Can you stop it?	Sometimes	Yes, once you are aware of it
What gets it started?	You may or may not contribute to it	Current situation seems like past abuse situation
How do you handle it?	You take evasive and protective action	You react identically to how you behaved during childhood maltreatment
How should you handle it?	Either perpetrator and partner tackle the problem together or injured party gets professional/police help	You must ask self: What evidence do I have that the other person meant harm?
How should significant other handle it?	Should work on herself never to be hurtful; should be patient during recovery	Should patiently clarify that her intensions were not mean; should never make fun of the person stuck in old memories

Unburdening yourself of victim thinking is liberating.

**(Tool 4) How to Overcome Victim Thinking
Reflect on This . . .**
Using the table above, can you tell whether you are, in fact,
a victim? How do you know?

This table is just a start. The next tool may surprise you.

Sometimes our bodies or our spirits aid us in identifying problems that we cannot solve consciously. Begin by noticing a bad feeling inside. For some people, that feeling may be physical, such as rapid breathing, a tight stomach, or pain somewhere. For other people, that feeling is emotional, such as sudden, unexpected anger, a welling up of sadness, a sense of hopelessness, a feeling of being trapped or frightened, or a disconnection from feelings altogether. Each person has a typical response to emotional distress.

Becoming aware of your reactions will help you resolve the issue of whether the victimization is happening in the here and now or something is just triggering victim thinking. Here's a story about Wanda whose stomach pain was a blessing.

Wanda came in for therapy with terrible stomach cramps. She had seen the medical doctor, but he could find nothing physically wrong. "I know it's me," she said. She then proceeded to tell the therapist about her son who was holding off going to college. She was okay with that, but her mother kept making her feel like a failure over it.

"And when do you get the stomach pain? Do you notice a pattern?" asked the therapist.

After a long moment of reflection, Wanda looked up, surprised. "Why, they always come within, say, ten minutes of talking on the phone to my

11

mother. Do you think there could be a connection?"

"What do you think?" asked the therapist.

"I guess there is," replied Wanda, sadly. "I wish I didn't get them, though."

"On the contrary," said the therapist. "Thank your wonderful stomach for being the red flag that you needed. After all, your stomach brought you here and now we can begin to figure out what exactly to say to your mother."

A symptom or pain may be a gift in disguise.

(Tool 5) How to Overcome Victim Thinking
Reflect on This . . .
Do you have unpleasant physical or emotional feelings when you talk to a particular person or when you discuss a particular subject? Have you noticed a difference in those feelings between times when you are clear that you are being mistreated from other times?

Next, take some slow, deep breaths to counteract the physical feeling and buy time for thinking through the situation. Deep breaths slow down the autonomic response system (pulse, blood pressure, heart rate, sweat—which are all signs of anxiety, stress, and imminent loss of emotional control). You will feel better just from that alone, although not better enough to have solved the problem.

Here's where emotional and physical healing meet.

(Tool 6) How to Overcome Victim Thinking
Get your autonomic nervous system under control by taking slow, deep breaths. It also buys time to think.

Now is the right time to download the additional tool I mentioned earlier just for buying this book. If you didn't already do it, please go to www. TheHealingIsMutual.com/download to get a 12 minute relaxation audio that I narrate. It begins with deep breathing.

Then, get very clear as to just exactly what triggered the response. Something in the current moment seemed like a terrible experience from childhood. What was it? When the baby came and Jean did not want sex, her tiredness and lack of warmth is what triggered Ricky. She reminded him—subconsciously—of his mother. It made him scared of being abandoned and rejected, and it made him angry too. The anger came from the sense of betrayal of their marriage vows: Here they pledged to be together forever and look at how she's already abandoning him! This wasn't the case, of course, but that's how Ricky felt. Jean's body language of fatigue in and of itself was a powerful trigger.

It is necessary for you to put a finger on exactly what your trigger is.

You can see from Ricky's experience that a person could be triggered when there is nothing really wrong.

Consider Wanda's story, above [Refer to pp. 11-12]. Suppose, for example, in Wanda's case her mother *used to* be a nervous person but has gone to therapy herself and has gotten control of her anxiety and is no longer mentioning her concerns over her grandson's college education. In other words, she is not in any way currently victimizing Wanda. However, the sound of her mother's voice may remain a trigger for Wanda.

Using the chart that precedes Tool 4, Wanda would consider Question 1: Is the mistreatment continuing? In giving it careful thought, Wanda would conclude that it is not; she was reacting to her mother's voice rather than what her mother said.

Getting clear can be a real challenge, but it's exhilarating to have done it.

(Tool 7) How to Overcome Victim Thinking
Reflect on This . . .

Get clear as to exactly what happened that triggered your automatic response. Pay *very close* attention to the actual words your partner used to see whether you are reacting to that person as a trigger from the past or whether something disturbing was said in the present moment.

When we are mired in victim thinking, separating the past from the present can become difficult. Our partner may actually look like or sound like or even use the same words as a parent used to. It's at this moment that you must ask yourself, "What evidence do I have that the past is repeating itself?" Be sure to *challenge the logic of your conclusion.*

Ask yourself over and over: Did she really mean to injure me? Because if your partner, lover, friend did not really mean it, you can then calmly tell her that it didn't come out right. You can explain what went wrong without absorbing all those victim wounds. Why take poison into yourself? You don't have to!

Let's meet Bernie. His father always said, "You'll never amount to anything." Unfortunately, that sentence has reverberated over and over in his brain all his life. When the least little thing went wrong, he could hear his father's voice saying, "You'll never amount to anything." To challenge and heal from this, he closely questioned the truth of this, pointing out to himself that he had raised good children and made a good living. Now, Melanie, his wife, innocently asked him what became of the promise his firm had given him for a pay raise. He could feel his throat constrict—that was his red flag—and took several deep breaths. He asked himself if Melanie meant to attack him. He answered in his mind, "Well, why did she have to bring it up?" He challenged this response by saying, "Well, she has a right to know our finances. It doesn't mean she is putting me down."

Start being in charge of your own feelings.

(Tool 8) How to Overcome Victim Thinking
Reflect on This . . .

What arguments can you use to challenge that voice that makes you feel like you are being injured? How can you question the validity of that voice? Whose voice is it, anyhow?

Note, please, that Bernie will probably not feel better at this moment. This is one of those times when emotions are so powerful that logic won't turn them around—yet. However, this really is a step toward healing. Getting your brain in charge of your *thoughts* always precedes *feeling* better. Don't make the mistake of assuming that things are not getting better because you still are reacting emotionally to the trigger. This is normal. When stressful events occur, the emotional part of the brain reacts very rapidly, often too rapidly for people to think clearly and respond well. It takes using several of the tools in this book to learn to calm down the emotional reactivity long enough for the thinking part of your brain to kick in. But at least now you can see that negative thoughts don't *have* to take permanent residence in your head.

You must brave this one out with lots of patience. If you have not been a patient person, now is the time to add *that* to your healing tools! Do it exactly the same way as you are learning to challenge negative thoughts. Ask yourself, "Can I really expect a quickie cure for a thinking process that took years or decades to develop?" Also notice the slight improvements in your patience level and give yourself credit for that. Pats on the back are good! And, of course, use Tool 6 and take deep breaths. That is an easy thing that will provide great benefit over time.

Bernie realized that it was ridiculous to hold Melanie responsible for his bad feelings. He accepted the fact that he just got triggered by her innocent question. His throat was still constricted and he didn't feel so

15

good. He went to the fridge for some cold water and that helped a little. He took some more deep breaths as recommended in Tool 6. He decided to go ahead and just answer her question as he kept repeating, "This is part of the process and I will feel better soon."

This process isn't easy but you can get through it—and come out ahead.

(Tool 9) How to Overcome Victim Thinking
Keep reminding yourself, "Feeling triggered is part of the process."
"Eventually, this won't trigger me anymore."
"Triggers are just automatic reactions. They're good to alert me in case something was wrong, but nothing is wrong right now."

When you have sweated over what was said and you remain uncomfortable, if it is possible to talk to your partner, try to air the problem so it is not festering inside. All the logic in the world does not equal the healing from a conversation in which your partner clarifies his meanings and intentions.

Bernie said to Melanie, "I think you know that I had a very demanding and belittling father, especially in the area of earning a living. I wish you would have been more tactful in how you brought up my pay raise." Melanie was astounded. "All I said was, 'What's the story on the pay raise?' How could that present a problem?" Bernie took another deep breath. "Well, why did you ask me at all? It sounded like you didn't believe I was going to get it." Again Melanie was astounded. "Wow," she said. "I'm always getting surprises from you. No, that was not the thought in my mind. I asked because, as you know, we are looking at Deanna's upcoming college tuition and I was starting to make some calculations. I just wanted some numbers to crunch, that's all." Bernie suddenly noticed the tension leave his throat. He let out a sigh. "Oh, that was it. I see," he responded. He proceeded to tell her the time frame for the pay raise.

In this scenario, even though Bernie had been successfully challenging his trigger reaction, he still could not figure out why his wife had asked him the question in the first place. Had his father asked that same question, he knew for sure that ridicule would be the next thing he'd hear. It will take Bernie and Melanie many weeks, perhaps months of having these kinds of conversations so as to really convince Bernie that Melanie is *always* coming from an innocent place, even when Bernie feels physiologically triggered.

Our partner—the person who seemed before like "the enemy," can be a tremendous source of healing.

(Tool 10) How to Overcome Victim Thinking
Without sounding aggressive, ask your partner what was behind her actions.

One thing that will give you a sense of control over what seems like a mugging by unexpected triggers is to start to catalogue what, exactly sets them off. For Bernie, it was conversations about money and success. For Wanda, it was the sound of her mother's voice. For Ricky, it was not being spoken to much and not reached out to. For Jean, it was having to hold up the fort all by herself. Knowing what your triggers are can help you in challenging them. Now that you have had at least one conversation with your partner about a recent triggering situation, you can begin your list. Write it down and have it handy. It will be a source of comfort to you when the next triggering situation occurs.

Control what was beyond your control by knowing what to expect.

(Tool 11) How to Overcome Victim Thinking
Reflect on This . . .
What triggers your victim response? Make a list of triggers. When the next situation occurs and you refer to your list, you can say, "Oh, yeah, that's one of my triggers." It will clue you in to the possibility that you are not being victimized.

17

In spite of these steps, a current situation may feel like an old, painful experience, almost like reliving a childhood trauma. For Ricky, the current situation felt just like the time his father walked out for good and his overwhelmed and unhappy mother stopped talking to him, not because she was angry at little Ricky, but just because she couldn't muster the energy to deal with a child.

One thing Ricky could have done was to separate the past from the present by telling himself again and again, "Jean is not my mother." Bernie could tell himself, "Melanie is not my father." Wanda could tell herself, "My mother has changed."

Have a mantra that anchors you to the present.

(Tool 12) How to Overcome Victim Thinking
Make statements to clarify the distinction between the past and the present, such as, "That was then; this is now," or, "My husband is not my father."

There are two skills that will propel you right past victim thinking very quickly. One is assertiveness. Assertiveness does *not* mean aggressiveness, quite the opposite. Being assertive is being straightforward in a civil, polite, and decent way. Assertiveness is called for when you feel you are being mistreated and want your needs met. By asking for what you want, the issue of being mistreated doesn't come up.

For example, if Jean's heart was really set on the paint job, she could have said to Ricky, "Look, I have no idea why you have been unpleasant to me these days. I'm tired, I work hard, I'm taking care of the baby, and you're not helping. But now, I've decided that I want to cheer myself up; I want to paint the living room. I would like blue. What's your choice of color?"

If he didn't answer, she could leave him a note. Maybe he is in the habit of totally tuning her out because he thinks that he's going to get "picked on" (his victim thinking). With a note, he cannot accuse her of inconsideration. That would be assertive for Jean—and highly considerate.

For Ricky, assertiveness might be asking her point blank what was going on instead of sulking. Or it could have been saying pleasantly to her, "When are we going to have sex again?"

As you can see in the example above, Bernie was assertive with Melanie when he began explaining to her his concerns. Would Wanda need any particular assertive strategy? I don't think so. Her mother was not being difficult; Wanda was triggered by the past.

One antidote to feeling like a victim is assertiveness.

(Tool 13) How to Overcome Victim Thinking
Reflect on This . . .
Are you assertive? Do you know how to be? Do you know, clearly, the difference between being assertive and being aggressive? What is it?

Now, please go to www.TheHealingIsMutual.com/download for a really potent tool. It is a one-sheet list of every major assertive response and most people find it to be one of the most effective tools in the toolbox.

This leads directly to the next tool to overcome victim thinking. What if, when Ricky asked when they would have sex again, Jean answered—again—that she was tired? Perhaps, just to make matters worse, she sounded a little annoyed at being asked the same question. Now, Ricky would have even more reason to go into victim mode. It would seem that this tool would backfire. Except that he can now use perhaps the hardest of all the tools: giving the benefit of the doubt.

People find this very difficult. When Bernie [Refer to pp. 14-16] was wondering what in the world made Melanie ask him about his pay raise, a way to help him feel better would have been to try to give her the benefit of the doubt. He could have asked himself in a way of curiosity rather than suspiciousness, "If her question was really innocent, why did she ask it?" See, the attitude with which you ask the question makes all the difference in the world.

In our story, Ricky needed to tell himself, "Don't jump to negative conclusions about what's in Jean's head. She *says* she's tired. Accept that." He would need to say this over and over again. Because he missed the closeness to Jean, giving her the benefit of the doubt might have opened him up to real solutions to his sexual frustration, too. He might have suggested just holding her hand, or perhaps, holding her as they fell asleep. The warmth of that encounter could have been deeply satisfying on other levels.

Giving the benefit of the doubt rids you of anger and frustration.

(Tool 14) How to Overcome Victim Thinking
Reflect on This . . .
Even when your partner acts badly, don't assume she meant to be mean; give the benefit of the doubt. Can you think of a recent example of something you could have interpreted in a more favorable way than you did?

Let's focus on Jean now. She needs the support of her husband, she's exhausted, she's also still pulling her weight financially even after having Goldie—and he is not there for her. Has she done anything wrong? No. However, she, too, fell prey to victim thinking.

You see, she really *was* a victim. Her husband was unhelpful; he demanded sex; he put her down in the restaurant; then he yelled at her. But she didn't have to wallow in her pain. That "poor me" attitude led her to paint their living room without making more effort to get Ricky's opinion on the color. If you are mistreated, don't get tempted into self-pity. Jean was on the right track to do something to lift her spirits but she needed a diversion that wouldn't have offended Ricky.

Take a cue from Jean and lift your spirits, but don't leave out your partner. Retain your dignity—and don't retaliate.

(Tool 15) How to Overcome Victim Thinking
Reflect on This . . .
One way to get out of feeling sorry for yourself is to focus on projects that could lift your spirits. What are yours?

Ending on an "Up" Note

Finishing up the session, the counselor asks, "Was the marriage always this bad or did it kind of creep up on you?"

Ricky has trouble focusing on the pain. He really doesn't want to be here having this conversation. He gives a short shrug. The therapist knows enough to try a different approach.

"How did you two meet?" she asks.

Ricky brightens. "Oh, man. She was the most beautiful girl there. My friend's sister introduced us. She was just so nice back then. The very day we met, she just seemed to open me up. We talked for hours, and I don't usually talk, you know." He looked expectantly at the therapist.

"Yes," she laughed, "I can tell." Realizing that she'd gotten quite a bit of information for that day, she brought the session to an end on a positive note with Ricky reminiscing about his and his wife's first meeting. This was a nice complement to Jean's comment about their early days.

When there's no therapist around, make a practice of ending discussions on an up note of your own. Say something positive, pay a compliment, invoke a good memory, express hope for the future.

Chapter Two
You Want to *Heal* Ricky, too?

I once had a client who took three parenting classes and one anger management class and passed them all with flying colors. He did great— in class. Except that he still yelled at his daughter. Then he came to see me and worked on healing from his own childhood where he was endlessly criticized. He didn't even realize that the relentless criticism he received amounted to abuse. There were many sessions of me reminding him to be nice to himself. He sort of got it, but he didn't, really.

Then one day, he had decided to ignore his daughter's misbehavior instead of yelling at her for it. That was a good step forward. On our next visit, he told me that, and I suggested instead of just ignoring the misbehavior, he find something positive to praise. That is, I was asking him to go from neutral to positive. I could see a light bulb go on over his head and he said, "My dad never praised me that way." Thoughtfully, he added, "So when I say something positive to my daughter, I can say something positive to myself as well."

What an a-ha experience that man had. Indeed, that is just what he did, and the yelling—for the first time—started to diminish.

Healing. That's what the approach in this book is all about.

Do people who injure others emotionally have to deal with their own controlling behaviors? Yes. But that is only one aspect of this approach. Do people who injure others emotionally have to deal with their own anger? Sure. But that, too, is only one area of focus.

The core idea in this book is that a person who is healing is open to change; one who isn't healing, isn't.

Healing is directed at the emotional centers of the brain (amygdala and others). With healing, an offensive person is receptive to techniques that connect these feeling parts of the brain with the parts that control rational thinking (cerebral cortex).

This is a hard sell. There are people who want to condemn Ricky instead. But that idea has flaws.

➢ The condemnation approach generates anger: Perpetrators become defensive and victims get angry. Instead of learning kindness, anger against them generates more anger at them and from them. That's what a fight is, isn't it? And you know that doesn't work.

➢ The condemnation approach is incompatible with healing. People being condemned put up more defenses on top of the ones already there. You can't get through to them.

Healing dismantles the protective shell abusers have built around their feelings. They learned to not feel their pain when they were mistreated, and because of that, they also can't feel other people's pain.

In contrast to condemnation, people who have started healing will know that they injured their loved ones. That is because once we help them identify and address their own pain, they can feel compassion. With compassion comes contrition and accepting responsibility. So, although it seems round-about, if we want those who injure others to feel compassion, contrition, and responsibility for the pain they have caused, they must heal first.

Ricky is *still* suffering from the trauma he experienced as a child. Certainly, not all mistreated children grow up to be mean adults. Some grow up to be targets again. Other sufferers grow up to lead sort of normal lives. The fact that not all wounded children grow up to be perpetrators does not change the fact that *all perpetrators were once victims.*

The goal is for adult offenders to become
• contrite people

- people who come to abhor mistreating another
- people who are kindly, compassionate, empathic, generous, sincere, and emotionally giving
- people who would not utter a word of blame or criticism again, let alone raise a fist in anger

If you have been mistreated in your marriage, part of your own healing will be to overcome your desire for revenge against your partner.

(Tool 16) Explain This . . .
Go over the beginning of this chapter. Why would a cruel and angry person need to heal first in order to become kind and compassionate?

Healing is necessary for both Jean and Ricky. Understanding how to get out of victim thinking is a strong beginning, but it is only the beginning.

PART II:

HOW WE HURT EACH OTHER –
AND HOW WE HEAL

From aggression to neglect, Part II covers it all: what violence really is, control, name calling, hypersensitivity, put-downs, blame, body language, yelling, and rejection. Part II defines hurtful behaviors and gives you tools to stop them. The tools will heal and empower you whether you have been hurt or you're doing the hurting.

Chapter Three
Do You Really Know What Violence Is?

Smitty had learned something from anger management. He was boiling right now but he did not push, shove, or punch his wife, Rachael. He knew violence is wrong. She'd learned too. She knew when it was time to leave an argument before it escalates. She headed for the door. Grinning, Smitty stood in the way. She couldn't get past him.

You might call that behavior aggressive, obnoxious, or bullying, but would you call it violent? I asked Murray Straus that question. He was the lead author of the book, *Behind Closed Doors,*[1] which got all of America thinking about domestic violence. He said, "In the case of psychological aggression, there are hundreds, perhaps even thousands, of different ways of doing it."[2] In his view, it is, at the very least, psychologically aggressive. Is it physical, too?

Let's see how the law defines "assault":

Assault and battery are intentional torts, meaning that the defendant actually intends to put the plaintiff in fear of being battered, or intends to wrongfully touch the plaintiff. The wrongful touching need not inflict physical injury, and may be indirect (such as contact through a thrown stone, or spitting). . .

An assault involves:

1. An intentional, unlawful threat or "offer" to cause bodily injury to another by force;

2. Under circumstances which create in the other person a well-founded fear of imminent peril;

3. Where there exists the apparent present ability to carry out the act if not prevented.

Note that an assault can be completed even if there is *no actual contact* with the plaintiff, and even if the defendant had no actual ability to carry out the apparent threat. For example, a defendant who points a realistic toy gun at the plaintiff may be liable for assault, even though the defendant was fifty feet away from the plaintiff and had no actual ability to inflict harm from that distance.[3]

Well, I have to tell you, I myself had never thought of *spitting* as an example of assault, but the law says exactly that.

"Assault," "aggression," or "violence" don't require contact for a person to feel threatened physically. The concept of violence lies on a continuum.

If we go back to Smitty, we could extend this concept to say that violence is something that takes away an individual's civil liberties. It is an exercise on the part of one individual to control the other against the other's will.

To earn trust, do not violate your partner's personhood.

(Tool 17) Reflect on This . . .
Are you violent? Do you take away someone's civil liberties? Is this done to you? Now that the topic is on the table, what do you plan to do about it?

Obviousness

From this perspective, an obvious physical attack isn't a *separate* act. It isn't different from other forms of restraint or control of freedom. Rather, all forms of violence fall on a scale from less obvious to more obvious. But the *result* is the same in each case: loss of civil liberties. When you don't realize it is happening to you, it's disconcerting to think that something was done to you, but you aren't clear why it's distressing. That's the sneaky part of the less obvious forms of violence.

The purpose of this chapter is to spell out that whole scale of what constitutes violent behavior. Then you will see how that ties into non-violent conflicts.

Any physical attack on a person's body is obvious violence. That includes, in addition to the acts listed at the beginning of this chapter, throwing objects at or near someone, biting, banging, or slamming a person, using an object to hit with, pinching, running into someone with a vehicle, kicking, kneeing, grabbing, and sitting on or putting pressure on someone in other ways, trapping, or tripping.

Less obvious would be various ways to imprison or limit freedom, such as by holding someone back, blocking an exit, or even keeping the keys to the car.

Smitty left for work with the slam of a door, leaving Rachael in the house two miles from the nearest grocery and no gas in the car. Smitty smirked as he remembered that he also took all the cash with him. "That'll teach her," he thought.

According to this perspective, withholding cash is violence.

What is the message from the person who controls the money so tightly that the partner cannot buy food or get to work? The message is, "I am in charge of *you*." If one person can regulate another's freedom to come and go so completely that the individual becomes virtually a prisoner, who knows what else this person can do?

This example fits Straus' use of the term "psychological aggression." It also fits the legal definition of assault in that it strikes fear into the heart of the victim. It fits my definition, too, because it limits freedom.

Healing can begin only when people are no longer violated.

> ### (Tool 18) Reflect on This . . .
> Name other ways that people can limit the personal freedom
> of others. Why would any of these behaviors be classified as
> "violence"? Are there any that have been done to you? Or
> that you have done to others?

*Rachael spent a good part of the day crying. She was still shaking from
her morning's encounter. She hadn't accomplished much by the time she
heard the front door slam. "So, are we going to fight again?" asked Smitty,
"because I am sick of it." He nodded his head toward the gun cabinet. "I
swear, the next time this happens, I'm giving up non-violence."*

Threats act the same way to limit freedom and they can be verbal or
implicit as in the story above.

*The evening was quiet; Rachael not wanting to stir up anything, remained
silent. At bedtime, Smitty grabbed for her and said, "Let's put this behind
us, c'mon, let's have sex." "I just can't," Rachael answered. "Not after
an awful day like today." "It was awful; I agree," replied Smitty. "That's
why this would fix it." "Not for me, it wouldn't," she answered. "Damn
you, woman," he said, growing angry. This time he grabbed her and had
his way with her. Rachael just cried, but that didn't change anything.*

This is a scenario of marital rape and constitutes violence. Every state
in the United States considers it a crime[4] and that is true in many other
countries as well.[5] Sex should always be consensual.

*When Smitty was done, he didn't feel any better. Nothing worked. He
got his way but so what? "I swear," he said watching Rachael continue
crying, "I'm just going to kill myself."*

Smitty's latest tactic is another way to exert control and therefore also constitutes violence. Threats intimidate whether they are made directly to the other person, or whether they imply harm to the person making them. They are all forms of violence—and can take various forms.

Frightening someone is a form of threat. The fear generated is a subtle message of, "If you think *this* is bad, just wait till you see what happens when you don't do what I say next time." So, making a show of driving dangerously falls into this category. Other examples include smashing something that is not near the person you want to frighten, slamming doors, punching walls, or attacking someone else.

Inflicting emotional pain is a form of threat. It gives the message: "I can injure you physically, just like I damaged you emotionally by hurting someone or something dear to you. So you better obey me." An obvious example of this would be harming or killing the children or pets of spouses. A less obvious example would be ripping up a piece of paper or photo that was precious to its owner. In both cases, the target of these attacks feels constrained to do what the aggressor wants in order to avoid further attacks or escalation to physical aggression; thus, they are attempts to limit physical freedom, making them examples of violence.

Violence Demonstrates a *Lack* of Control

If the essence of violence is limiting another person, the next question is: Why do it? This question is especially pertinent because being violent hurts the violent person nearly as much as it does the target of the violence. There's absolutely nothing beneficial about it for violent people because:

➢ The more violent they are, the less likely they are to get what they want.
➢ They are not happy with themselves.
➢ The more they exert control over others, the *less* they feel in control of the situation.

People who lash out have poor relationships with those they attack and derive little satisfaction from their relationships. Accomplishments in other areas of life are overshadowed by the bleakness of the relationship with the people closest to them.

Attempts to constrain others stem from a lack of skill at gaining voluntary agreement from the other person. True control is getting that voluntary agreement, and that kind of control is a happy experience for both people.

Ricky, Jean, and Their Future

Neither Ricky nor Jean understood true control. Neither knew how to get what they wanted from the other person. Ricky felt badly about who he was as a person and he was, indeed, unhappy. He would assume that his unhappiness came from Jean's mistreatment of him, an error in logic and understanding that made him feel *entitled* to be angry at her. His anger did not get him what he wanted anyway.

Although Ricky indicated that there had been no physical violence, statistics show that once there is one episode of physical aggression, other episodes will follow more frequently. For example, in 1974, Murray Straus, a professor at the University of New Hampshire, demonstrated that venting not only does not "get out" anger, but it actually increases it.[6] This initial research led to the first large-scale national survey of verbal and physical aggression.[7] Other researchers have shown that over time, psychological or verbal aggression is a good predictor of physical violence.[8]

The worst part of verbal venom is that it is so insidious. If you grew up in a house of yelling, yelling is normal for you. If you grew up in a house of put-downs or blame, ditto. It's for that reason that many people don't even realize that they are being injured.

This is a real shame because the number of people who are verbally attacked is huge. Consider that the most recent data, obtained from the National Domestic Violence Survey done in 2000, show that 1.3 million women and 835,000 men are physically assaulted by an intimate partner every year.[9] Since every case of domestic violence includes a verbal component, there are at least that many people suffering from verbal abuse. But we know that verbal abuse is far more prevalent than physical abuse. So the above numbers are just a baseline, a starting point in tallying the amount of injury due to verbal aggression. In fact, as we become more aware of workplace harassment and school bullying in which there is no physical component, we get a glimpse of the enormity of the picture.

What about You?

It's time to face yourself; you can do it. And you can get past it. Please go through the following chart and check off—with honesty—items of violence that you have experienced, either as abuser or recipient. Cleaning the wound out is the necessary step toward its healing. You will next have to make a commitment never to exercise any of these forms of violence again if you were the aggressor.

If you were the victim, you will have to take action to protect yourself. You should call the police if you are afraid. You might consider going to a shelter or another safe space that is unknown to your partner if this could happen again. You certainly should let your partner know that there is a problem to be worked on. Don't be a target a second time.

Can you look in the mirror? See the strength you didn't know you had.

(Tool 19) Check the ones that apply to you from the following list

most obvious forms	what you did/do	what was/is done to you
hitting		
hitting with object		
punching		
kicking		
shoving		
burning		
bruising		
tripping		
throwing objects at		
slamming		
biting		
pinching		
driving into		
kneeing		
grabbing		
sitting on		

more subtle forms	what you did/do	what was/is done to you
verbal threats and/or gestures		
possession of guns, weapons		
holding someone back		
blocking an exit		
keeping the car keys		
maintaining no gas in car		
marital rape		
destroying cherished possessions, pets		
harming someone's child(ren)		

Verbal Violence

Next on our continuum of aggression is what researchers have called verbal violence.[10] Name-calling, put-downs, implications through body language, yelling, blaming, and criticizing are examples. Their injury is more subtle but just as devastating as physical violence.

Verbal violence is:
➤ More pervasive than all other abuse

> ➤ Harder to recognize as being wrong
> ➤ More likely to be transmitted to your children than physical abuse

If you ask the question, "Why?" about each of the above, the answer is the same: Physical violence is so obviously wrong that adults who were mistreated in childhood are more likely to say, "I'm not going to do that to *my* family." But when throwing darts is part of general conversation, children growing up with it think it's normal. And the subtler it is, the harder it is for people to see that it is wrong and cruel. So there's more of it and it spreads to the next generation.

The pain that it inflicts gets into the soul. With domestic violence, the recipient can always make an excuse for the attacker, like, "He lost his temper." But once nasty words are out, that's it; there's no going back. They affect the essence of a person, where they tear it to shreds. This is how harsh language affects relationships:

> ➤ It doesn't accomplish what the individual wanted.
> ➤ It wounds the targeted person *more* than its physical counterpart.
> ➤ It makes your partner want to get away from the wounds you create. (Therefore, it may lead to addictions or suicide.)
> ➤ It creates roadblocks to clear communication.
> ➤ It stands in the way of trust and intimacy.
> ➤ It may end up destroying the relationship.
> ➤ It can lead to being attacked back.
> ➤ It can cause hate.
> ➤ It can—and often does—escalate to physical violence.

Finally, at the very opposite end of the injury spectrum is the *absence* of doing something—neglect. Neglect is emotional abuse because it is tormenting to the neglected party. Someone who enjoys reading the newspaper or watching TV at breakfast when a partner would rather visit doesn't realize the walls that he is building that way and what the emotional consequences are to the other person. Although there is no violence in neglect, it may lead to violence.

Maybe it will be easier to understand it by looking at how it affects children.

A neglected child seems on the surface to be free to do anything, so how can that be an example of taking away civil rights? The answer is that her parents' neglect means they didn't teach her life skills and coping mechanisms for dealing with stress and adversity. It also means that they didn't provide her with love, warmth, and helpful feedback on how she was handling her life. Because of these gaps in filling her emotional needs, she is not only unhappy, but she has no tools with which to pursue happiness.

It is sad but not surprising that according to research at the Rochester Institute of Technology, "Suicide is the third leading cause of death for fifteen to twenty-four-year olds and the sixth leading cause of death for five to fourteen-year olds." The same researcher points out that when facing problems, "Most children become silent and do not open up to the parents about what is wrong and what is bothering them."[11]

This is one way that child neglect can lead to violence. The violence may also be deferred until adulthood.

Just as the neglected child is left without tools to cope, the neglected partner does not know why the cold partner is acting that way; therefore she has no way to remedy the problem. Without a remedy, the neglected partner feels despair. While it should be true that an adult will have better resources than a child to cope with this despair, the despair of adults can be as devastating as it is to children.

Be strong and recognize that you may have hurt those you love.

(Tool 20) Reflect on This . . .
Given all that, do you really want to continue to inflict suffering?

Using aggressive methods to control others not only doesn't work, but an honest appraisal would conclude that the controller doesn't even feel in control.

Stop being controlling and get real control.

(Tool 21) Reflect on This . . .
Do you feel in *control* of your life?

The next chapter takes the subject of control into another area where people often miss it.

Chapter Four
Power and Voice

Have you ever thought about who has the voice in your family and how they got it?" When that person speaks, others listen. How did that happen?

Betty started to explain in some detail why she was able to get free to go out on an errand her husband wanted. She wanted to give him the message that her being able to go out was something of a sacrifice of her time. But, as she was talking, he cut her off. "Okay. Okay," he said. "Get to the point."

Why should she get to the point? Because he decided? But she decided that she wanted him to hear the whole thing. Who is right? Who decides? Does he have the right to dictate how much she should speak? Does she have the right to force him to listen to that whole story?

In a healthy relationship, people take turns getting it "their" way: Sometimes *he* has to listen and sometimes *she* has to cut to the chase. When it's unbalanced, there is emotional damage going on. Either she is controlling him by forcing him to always listen, or he is insulting her by rudely making her cut short what she wanted to say.

How do you convert the above scenario into a healthy give-and-take? The answer is manners. He should have said, "I'm not up to a long version. Is that okay?" And provided he doesn't make this request all the time, it would be fine. The idea is to have a balance of power in the relationship. This keeps it from being concentrated in only one person's hands.

Balancing the power is healing.

(Tool 22) How to Give Your Partner Voice
Take turns. Also, ask if it's okay to cut it short or to interrupt.

41

Betty also could have been sensitive to his mood. She could have said, "I'd like to explain the whole thing to you, okay?" And provided she doesn't do that all the time, that, again, preserves a balance of power.

Build trust by relinquishing power.

```
(Tool 23) Reflect on This . . .
Who calls the shots in your house? Who does all the talking?
Who explains what's what to the insurance man? Is that the
way you want it to be? What can you say to make changes?
```

The Aggressor Loses out

What the bully doesn't realize is that by being overly controlling in this fashion, he is actually not getting *his* needs met. After all, when he gets his way all the time, he is in a very lonely place: He is not "part of." That is typical for aggressors: They are not happy.

This fact is empowering for the one who is left out and she should use it to regain balance. The person without a voice needs to take action when the one with the power won't give it up. Don't argue. Instead, when one person always dominates conversations, the other person must state something to the effect of:

> "When you have it your way all the time, it makes *you* alone. Do you see that? We have drifted apart because of this. Is that where you want us to be?"

For relationships to prosper, not only should the recipients be assertive, but bullies must realize that their behavior is causing them to lose the very thing they both wanted—a relationship.

When just one person in the relationship has the voice, the person whose voice was lost:

➤ Resents the one holding the power
➤ Has no joy in the relationship (which may eventually lead to *no* relationship)
➤ Loses touch with himself

The last one is significant. We know who we are by what we say. If you never expressed your opinion, wouldn't you lose touch with what it is after a while? A person's whole identity can be lost just because they aren't allowed to complete a thought.

For the perpetrator, the outcome is no better:
➤ Loneliness
➤ A perpetual bad mood
➤ Nothing and no one pleases her

Bottom line: When one person has all the answers, neither one is happy. It's destructive. And it's lonely.

Control Covers More Than Getting the Last Word

Such a power differential takes place in many aspects of the relationship. It goes beyond control of ideas to include:

➤ Control of place—which occurs when the controller has to know where the controlled partner is at all times and controls all movements
➤ Control of money—which could be so intense that a partner may not have food to eat while the controller is recklessly throwing parties
➤ Control of contacts—so that the controlled partner's conversations and friends are limited. Sometimes this is accomplished by making fun of the friend or family member; sometimes by being jealous of the friend's attention; sometimes by acting sorry for oneself because the controller didn't get as much attention as that friend
➤ Control of behavior—compelling the victim to do what the controller wants—no matter how opposed to it the partner is—from being the chief cook and bottle washer to submitting to forced sex

The process of achieving this level of control may involve threats, intimidation, name-calling and other ugliness, but it certainly doesn't have to be that way. Control can be achieved simply by arguing, but there are even subtler ways to accomplish the same goal. I counseled a couple once in which the husband was too "nice." All he wanted to do was "take care of" his wife, but her life became so restricted that she was emotionally suffocated.

Take for example Sydney. She's married to Arthur, who has been diagnosed with Attention Deficit Hyperactivity Disorder. Indeed, he is quite disorganized. Sydney would tell him frequently how to organize his papers, but she wouldn't stop there—she would organize them. You'd think that was sweet and helpful, but Arthur wouldn't be able to find anything. No matter how many times he would tell her he can't find anything, she would continue to organize him. This would include throwing out what might look to her like scrap, but on which he had written phone numbers that he felt he needed.

Manny would control Sylvia differently. He would call her when she was supposed to be through with work to find out when she was leaving. Then he would clock how long she was gone and would question her if she came home five minutes later than it usually takes. He explained that he was "worried" about her well-being, but she felt stifled.

Ed would ask Cheryl what she was doing, and then, no matter what it was, he'd give her several suggestions on how to do it. He never explicitly said that she was incompetent, but she started to feel that way. If she wasn't incompetent, why did he keep giving her suggestions? Didn't he believe she had the skills to do anything?

Taking control can be a form of bondage—for both people.

(Tool 24) Reflect on This . . .
Sometimes people take control by doing all the *thinking* in the family. Does someone in your family do that? Come up with as many examples as you can.

Another method of controlling is to feel hurt all the time—what I've been calling "playing victim." If everything I do hurts you, I will just stop doing things on my own. Pretty soon, I'm doing nothing—except what you have specifically "permitted."

Get out from under the shackles of playing victim.

> **(Tool 25) Reflect on This . . .**
> Do you or your partner control the other by playing victim?
> Can you come up with examples?

Here's another way to be controlling: by asking the other to take control. Here's an example I learned from my husband. It goes like this:

Me: What do you want for supper?
Husband: Anything, dear. Anything you want is fine.
Me: Well, what I don't want is to decide. I'm tired of being in charge of thinking about dinner. I've got clients to see and I'm still working on my book. I don't want to be in charge of dinner.
Husband: Well, I don't know. . . .

See how that goes? So he gets me to do all the thinking! On the surface, I'm in control. But really, he put me there by not being in control. People who love psychobabble like to call this being "passive aggressive." Call it what you want, but I'm not interested in thinking about dinner.

Luckily for me, I figured this one out and didn't do anything about dinner. Some hours later, I complained to him that I was hungry.

Him: Well, what did you decide about dinner?
Me: I didn't decide. I told you I wanted you to decide.
Him: Well, I don't know.
Me: I don't like "I don't know." It doesn't taste good.
Him: [looking at computer; not into conversation] Well, I don't.

Me: [very good at this game] I think I deserve more effort than that. Oh, well. I'll just get back to my work. I'm sure you'll come up with something because I know how much you tell me you love me and want to take care of me.

He has learned. He usually does.

This game can involve many different areas of life. Let's call it being-in-control-by-not-taking-charge. A frequent one is not standing up to your abusive parents so that your partner is stuck with what they dish out. Another one is not spending time on what the kids need to do so your partner is the one who makes sure the homework gets done and they get to bed on time. It's a way of making your partner do all the work so you can wiggle out of responsibilities.

Finally, you can control someone else's emotions by taking this not-being-in-charge role. If you need to take responsibility for the kids' bedtime or for picking up the dry cleaning or for telling your parents you can't be with them for dinner next Sunday and you don't do it—again—then your partner will, predictably, become angry with you. Now that he is angry with you, you can take a Holier-Than-Thou position and say, "See? I'm not the only one who loses my temper!" But, of course, you actually manipulated him into that anger by not doing what you were supposed to. (That doesn't justify the anger, by the way. It just clarifies how it came about.)

Watch out for control by not shouldering responsibility.

> ### (Tool 26) Reflect on This . . .
> Do you get stuck being in charge more often than you want?
> Do you feel like your anger got manipulated?

How to Give up Control

If you think you may be controlling, it is time to take a look at this. There are seven ways to release control; gravitate to those that feel most comfortable.

Sydney [Refer to p. 44] *realized that by cleaning Arthur's desk, she wasn't being "too nice"; she was taking away from him something that made him unique. She couldn't stand the mess, herself, but somehow needed to let Arthur be himself. She gently closed his office door whenever she went by and left the mess intact. She suddenly grasped that she now had 15 extra minutes to herself every time she did that.*

Healing the spirit entails acceptance of—and appreciation for—life as it is.

(Tool 27) How to Release Control #1
Learn to not "do" or expect others to do. Just "be." Learn how to just be by taking scenic walks, learning to paint, draw, play an instrument, or do other art forms. Just sit and watch the scenery, read poetry, meditate.

Ed had a busy medical practice with a full slate of quality personnel; yet, in the past, he couldn't seem to let them all do their jobs. He invariably took an extra 30 seconds to comment on their work. He recently noticed that his employees looked strained. He decided to stop poking his nose into their tasks. This was very difficult; after all, his income depended on how they did their work. He compromised by instituting a quarterly review for himself of what needed to be done. Three months later, he took a few weekends to go through all the books, records, and logs. He jotted down who made the fewest errors and decided to give those people a year-end bonus. He also sent them heads-up letters to that effect. Soon, he noticed employees who had been slacking were making more effort—all without him backsliding to little remarks and reminders.

"I need to try this at home," he thought. "I'm full of advice for my wife before she has a chance to come up with her own ideas." Ed started to hold back his advice at home. Sure enough, he could see that things went quite smoothly without his two cents. The following year, he hired a firm to do the time-consuming audit he had done at work and realized that the time and stress he saved were well worth the cost. "Luckily," he mused, "my wife doesn't need an audit! She really is a competent person." A sense of peace descended over Ed that he hadn't known in years.

Start practicing acceptance with friends or employees, then your partner.

> **(Tool 28) How to Release Control: #2**
> Develop other friendships and enjoy all of them; practice letting others be who they are.

Healing the spirit requires seeing the good in your life.

> **(Tool 29) How to Release Control: #3**
> Practice reflecting each night before bed on the good that is in your life. Focus specifically on each good thing and linger over it for a few moments, visualizing its goodness in your life.

Ed was so pleased with the outcome of letting go that he decided to go one better. He wondered if, left to their own devices, his employees might come up with great ideas that he had never thought of. Again, this was difficult for him. He instituted an anonymous suggestion box for improving efficiency and effectiveness. He was surprised at the high quality of ideas he got. He sent around a memo expressing his pleasure, and, sure enough, once the recommendations were implemented, he saw productivity improve even more.

You can't force flowers to bloom but you can prepare the soil.

(Tool 30) How to Release Control: #4
Create opportunities for others to perform without your micromanagement—but with your encouragement—and see the quality of their work improve.

When Manny and Sylvia [Refer to p. 44] *would fight, he felt awful. Sylvia came across something about "controlling men" online and she unexpectedly flared up at her husband. "I'm sick and tired of being tagged like an experimental animal who sends back radio signals where ever it is," she said vehemently. "I only want the best for you," he declared unconvincingly. "No, you want to control me," she announced.*

At first, such an attack on his motives made him angry, but in the darkness of the night, he gave it some thought. Maybe it was true. Maybe he feared one day she just wouldn't be there; she'd leave. But why? Why would she do that? "Maybe I'm not good enough for her," he thought. Manny didn't know where that crazy thought came from, but he worked up the courage to tell it to her. Sylvia's good heart reached out to him. "That's silly," she said. "Where did you get that from?" Where, indeed? People more often than not are not in touch with their subconscious feelings—which often originate from childhood experiences—but they can still address their behavior and attitudes. He realized that his controlling behavior came from his fears of Sylvia leaving. Manny knew this thinking was detrimental and he resolved to change it.

Practice self-love.

> **(Tool 31) How to Release Control: #5**
> Appreciate yourself. Sometimes control is the result of not believing you are lovable or capable yourself, so you think you have to force someone into acting loving or caring. Reflect on your good qualities and concentrate on bringing them out more often. Making a list really helps because once it's in writing, you can't deny its truth.

Are you worth being nice to yourself?

> **(Tool 32) How to Release Control: #6**
> Create a "pamper" list for yourself and select one item on it to pamper yourself with every once in a while. Often, people who control others are quite uncomfortable giving to themselves, but it is healthy to get used to caring for and comforting oneself.

De-stressing is part and parcel of healing.

> **(Tool 33) How to Release Control: #7**
> Notice what de-stresses you and start doing it more often. Make a list and keep it on the refrigerator to remind you.

How to Be Strong

The damaged partner can do a lot to prevent her partner from being tempted into controlling again. She needs two critical tools: to understand *boundaries* and to be *assertive* in sticking to them.

➢ Boundaries

How much will you take? That is the question of the day. And that is the essence of setting up boundaries. I think making this point will be easiest to see if we start with examples of parents and children.

Scene: A little kid, maybe four, wanted candy. She was in the store with mom. She screamed. Mother ignored her. She screamed some more. Mother said, "No." Her screaming crescendoed until finally the mother gave in.

Scene: Another little kid, another mother. This mother also said "No," but the child kicked her hard. The mother laughed self-consciously when the other shoppers stared at her. She turned to the little girl and said, "That's not nice," and then bought her the candy.

Scene: A third child wanted candy. A third mother. The mother said, "No, honey, not before dinner." The child whined and the mother smiled at the child and said, "I know you want it. I'll bet you're getting hungry thinking of dinner. I'm so sorry, but we're not getting candy." The child made the mistake of screaming. Mom's eyebrows went up. She stared at him, narrowing her eyebrows and frowning. "Mommy is very unhappy with your behavior. There will be no dessert tonight." The child began to cry and mom stared at him, raising her hand into a stop signal. "You'd better stop before you have to have an early bedtime also." He stopped.

The first two moms had weak boundaries. Essentially, they let the army invade. If you were to ask them, "If your child wants candy before dinner, do you think they should have it?" they'd say, "No, of course not." But they both gave in. The second mother had no clue that she was teaching her child that violence is all right if you want something badly enough. Only the third mother knew what she wanted and stuck to it. Note that she did it without sinking down to the child's level; she neither screamed nor hit.

Having boundaries means being really clear about how you want to be treated. A client of mine went out on a first date with a new man. At dinner, he suggested that she shouldn't chew gum during the meal. Whoa!

Talk about an infringement of boundaries. Here he was, a total stranger, minding her business. "But," she protested to me when I expressed my concern, "he was nice." "No," I explained, "he wasn't. He's not your mother. There is no reason for him to teach you table manners. That was rude because he had no sense of boundaries." This point stands even though you may think that chewing gum at dinner is rude. Mr. Nice's option would be to not go out with her again. Two wrongs, after all, do not make a right.

Lillian was a nervous person. She thought she needed Matthew's help for so many things that she would have been capable of had she practiced doing them herself. He called her at the end of his day to say he would have to be home late because a meeting with an important client unexpectedly came up. Matthew was in the middle of the meeting when Lillian could no longer stand the fact that he wasn't home yet, helping her with the kids. She texted him three times in 10 minutes. Finally, he had to excuse himself from his client and go to another room to reply to Lillian that he was not going to be available just yet.

He got home after eight o'clock that night. Lillian was fuming. He reminded her that he had given her a courtesy call to let her know he was going to be late and then told her she would have to get a grip on herself for times when this happens and not interrupt meetings.

Lillian invaded her husband's boundaries in this scenario. Matthew had few options at the time; however, he made it clear later where his boundaries were.

How much do other people step on your toes?

(Tool 34) Reflect on This . . .
Are your boundaries strong? Are you crystal clear on what you will and won't take? Do you stick to it? Can you give some examples? What do you need to help you with this exercise?

Power and Voice

➢ Assertiveness

Now, I'd guess those first two mothers knew what they wanted, but they just didn't know how to stick to it. Sticking to it is called being "assertive." This is not to be confused with being aggressive. The difference is that while being assertive means being firm, it is also quiet and respectful. The assertive person is in full control of the situation with a minimum of effort, unlike the aggressive person who has to pull out all the stops to gain control. The aggressive or violent person actually lacks control. He does not know how to get what he wants using normal means. But the assertive person does.

Shaindy screamed at Yossi because he didn't handle the children's bedtime the way she thought it ought to be. They ended up in bed an hour late. Yossi looked Shaindy in the eye and said, "Stop screaming. I deserve better."

Harry, Marcia's boss, decided to foist some extra work on her for the fifth time that week just as everyone was leaving for the day—again. The other times, she did stay. After all, she wanted to give the impression of being a gung-ho worker—even though her job description said nothing about overtime. But she had finally begun to feel that he was taking advantage of her, especially since she was not paid for the additional hours. She gave a lot of thought to handling it, and then she said, "Harry, I really appreciate your confidence in me to be able to handle such a workload. And the truth is, I enjoy getting the extra work; it's a great challenge. Can you give me several days' notice when you want me to work after hours in the future?"

John is frantic. He has, as usual, lost his papers. He needs them for a meeting tomorrow. In addition, he has a dozen errands to run. "Susan," he calls out, "Help me please! I need you to run to the bank, find my papers, get that order delivered . . ." Susan works full time and does well over fifty percent of the child care. "Gee, John, I'm sorry, but I can't do your errands. I'm already saddled with too much to do. Maybe if you just take a minute to relax and let your mind go, you'll remember where you left those papers."

Many people ask me what to do when the assertive response doesn't work because the partner won't take "no" for an answer and becomes aggressive. That's where we must loop back into the other methods we will discuss as we go forward, such as time out and giving constructive criticism. And of course, that's why this book was written for both the injured party and aggressor.

For a little help with assertiveness, take a look at the assertive chart I created. If you haven't already done so, please go to www.TheHealingIsMutual.com/download.

Build up your assertive muscle through practice.

(Review Tool 13) Reflect on This . . .
Are you assertive? Can you stick to your goals without yelling when there's opposition?

Jean and Ricky

Where do Jean and Ricky come in? As long as Ricky is an angry man, the anger will forever control Jean. She will always hold herself back from saying/doing something out of fear. That is bad not only for Jean but for Ricky. He will lose her as a true partner.

Ricky's moodiness and neglect controlled Jean right from the beginning. His moodiness made her afraid to approach him. Although she "tried," she obviously didn't try hard enough because, in the end, she never did tell him about the painting project. The result was not only that *she* was miserable and fearful, but *he* got left out—the very thing he felt badly about from the beginning. The irony is that in the beginning, she did not willfully leave him out; she'd just had Goldie, their baby. But in the end, she did because she didn't know how to approach him.

When a partner is cold, moody, blaming, or neglectful, it exerts just as much control as a beating. Ricky prevented the very thing he wanted: Jean's attention. So they both lost out.

Memo to bullies: The more you control, the worse you make it for yourself.

(Tool 35) Explain This . . .

Explain, in your own words, how Ricky's moodiness worked against him.

I don't want you to think that Ricky's control through sulking, appearing cold, and being unhelpful rendered Jean unable to get out of the situation. If Jean had been stronger, the control would have disappeared. Don't forget, a lot of this is purely psychological. She felt under his control because of his coldness, and she was therefore afraid to bring up anything for fear of making it worse. But the truth is that a frank and honest conversation could have made it better. Her fear is her own.

Let's look at just a few of the tools we've covered to see how Jean could have gotten out from under Ricky's control.

Tool 13: Assertiveness.

Jean could have made up her mind that the living room was going to be painted, no matter what. She could have approached Ricky personally, on the phone, by email, with a note, or by text message. I've found that arguing couples can be more rational in written messages than in person because not being together has a cooling effect.

Tool 26: Not shouldering responsibility.

It seems that Jean has to do all the mental management of the family. By being a victim, Ricky gets out of it. Jean could have said to him, "I'm tired, as I told you. I'm not only tired of the night feedings and going to work, but I'm tired of thinking about how to cheer myself up when my husband isn't helping. Now I'm giving that job to you. Think of how to make me feel better."

That would certainly have opened up a discussion.

Note that this chapter on "Power and Voice" and the previous chapter, "Do You *Really* Know What Violence Is?" are related. They're both about control. The subtle forms of control presented in this chapter, like Sydney organizing Arthur's papers and Lillian texting her husband during a meeting, are not violent. The people involved were not screaming or angry. Sydney was sweet and Lillian was a nervous wreck. Yet they are in essence no different than Smitty keeping the gas tank empty and holding onto the family cash when he left for work. Control is control and it's all bad.

The remaining chapters in Part II are about highly common and damaging ways that people misuse the power of speech.

Chapter Five
Name-Calling Is No Big Deal--Or Is It?

Sally and Fred had gotten into it once again.

"You idiot," he exclaimed. "Can't you do anything right?"

Well, the truth is, she had made a mistake. She had her hands full with packing to visit their children at college, continuing to run her business, and help Fred with his own stuff. So she paid her credit card bill four days late. And it lowered the score. A lot. That didn't help as they were about to lease a new car.

Here are some questions that people ask about name-calling:
➢ What's wrong with name-calling anyway?

➢ Why can't people just take a joke?

➢ If I'm mad at someone, shouldn't I be able to express my feelings so that the person knows she did something wrong?

Let's explore each.

What's Wrong with Name-Calling?

In a marriage, you are supposed to be equal partners. Right? However, the person who pins a label on another person is taking power away from the other person. (That is a reason why, as a marriage and family therapist, I do not believe in giving people a diagnosis—it, too, is a process of labeling people. It gives me power beyond the power inherent in the therapeutic relationship.)

In calling Sally an "idiot," Fred took away her equality; he became "smarter."

Marriages are not supposed to be power struggles. In fact, if I call you *anything* except something you would agree with or a compliment, it's rude, wrong, and hurtful.

It may be that Fred did not intend to hurt Sally. It may be that he has no interest in wielding power over her. The Freds of this world simply want to *reclaim lost power.*

Fred may believe Sally has hurt him. When abusive people feel hurt, they feel like the other person has put them down. I can hear Fred saying, "If my wife really loved me and respected me, she would not have done that." They leave no room for human error, no room for being overloaded with several priorities, and no room for giving the benefit of the doubt [Refer to Tool 14, p. 20]. Here we meet our old friend, victim thinking. Watch out for how victim thinking leads directly to much of the abuse described in the next few chapters. When a person feels like a victim, the only way to reclaim their lost power is to get back at the other person.

How did Fred become a victim thinker? Fred was seven. He stood behind the door, wanting to know. "You idiot!" exclaimed his father. "How could you do that?" Fred's heart was beating rapidly. Oh, boy, he'd get it if they discovered him here. He tiptoed back to his room. He shut the door carefully, lay down, but couldn't fall asleep. He wasn't the target—this time. He was almost relieved.

Fred felt like a perpetual victim, like Ricky. Ever afraid of being called on the carpet, he learned from his father that the best defense is a good offense. Unfortunately, victim thinkers underestimate how much such attacks hurt. What they're doing is overkill; the pain of their name-calling far exceeds the pain they fancy they received from their partner.

To move beyond a toxic way of relating, we must distinguish bad from good.

(Tool 36) Obvious Name-Calling: Checklist

Here's a list of nasty labels that often get pinned on people. (The ones on this list are printable. You're familiar with all the ones that aren't, I'm sure.) Are you guilty of any of these, or are you the one that got labeled?

➢ Stupid
➢ Dumb
➢ Idiot
➢ Slut
➢ Whore
➢ Imbecile
➢ Lazy
➢ Selfish
➢ Space cadet
➢ Gold-digger
➢ Loser
➢ Opportunist
➢ Brown-noser
➢ Girl (to a male)
➢ Bad
➢ Klutz
➢ Filthy
➢ Dirty
➢ Sloppy
➢ Pig
➢ Used up
➢ Washed out
➢ Wasted
➢ Ugly
➢ Witch
➢ Others you've given or received . . .

Whether you're the giver or receiver, it's got to STOP now. These are so bad, so horrendous, that you should never utter or hear them again. If you are either the giver or receiver of anything like any on this list, learn the most effective tool in all the anger management classes right now: Time out.

If you have received this sort of onslaught, let your partner know *before there's another problem* that this can't and won't continue and that you will leave *without a word* the next time it either happens or is about to happen. Tell your partner *now* that leaving is not meant to be insulting and is not a way of avoiding discussion. It is a way of *avoiding emotional harm*. Then, when the moment comes, request your tormentor leave, or if you are afraid your partner will not leave or it will escalate, then you should leave.

If you have been dishing it out, then you, too, can take the initiative to leave. Let your partner know that you are doing it to prevent escalation.

"Now listen to me," Sally said in a serious tone of voice, staring Fred straight in the eye. "You will NOT talk like that to me. Ever. Right now, you take a walk. Get some fresh air. Leave. You offended me; you need to leave." She kept staring at him. She was very angry. Somewhere inside, she was also scared. But she had to do this.

Fred stared at her for a few moments, and then turned and stomped out of the house.

He came back two hours later. He said nothing, afraid that he would blow up. But Sally took the lead. "You did the right thing to leave when you did, rather than hurt my feelings again," she said. "Next time, you need to leave BEFORE anything comes out of your mouth. Do you understand?"

Fred muttered, "Yes." Nothing more was said because it was obvious to both of them that they were still angry.

Three days later, when several pleasant things had happened to them and both were in a decent mood, Sally asked Fred, "Are you prepared to take a time out next time you feel like being nasty so you don't hurt my feelings?" "Yes," he said. "I don't want to hurt you."

Build respect by not saying the things that hurt.

(Tool 37) How to Take a Time Out

1. Agree ahead of time, before there is an "issue," that the angry one has to leave the house in order to prevent abuse.

2. Neither person should try to finish the conversation or feel insulted by the time out.

3. Attempt to be gracious and say, "I'm taking a time-out" in a neutral tone of voice.

4. Leave until you are totally cooled down.

Gray Areas

It's possible for something that sounds totally innocent to an observer to be a "label." Here's a good rule to know if something is ill-intended: (1) If it is an exaggeration or completely misses the boat in knowing where the other person is coming from; and (2) in spite of being corrected, you or your partner repeat the same mistake many times.

Bill Black is the president of a small company. His wife, Diane, frequently calls him "Bill Gates."

That's mean. It's not only factually incorrect, but it does not respect what he actually does. It's as if Diane was saying, "Anything less than being Bill Gates is no good and nothing special." It's sarcastic; it's name-calling.

So why would Diane do that anyway? Perhaps she's frustrated because he's not earning enough. Perhaps she's annoyed that he spends so much time at work, acting as if he were Bill Gates. Perhaps she thinks that he

61

spends too much money on charity. Who knows?

And that is one of the biggest problems with name-calling: The speaker *never communicates what the problem really is*. So, in addition to being hurtful, it's also pointless.

What else could Diane do? Easily, she could just tell Bill what's bugging her in plain language. She could, for instance, say, "I don't like the amount of time you spend away from home on business." Nothing could be plainer than that.

Maybe she tried that and Bill didn't listen, but, clearly, the name-calling hadn't worked either.

When you speak, know what you're doing.

(Tool 38) How to Tell if it's Name-Calling
1. It's an exaggeration OR misses the boat completely.
2. The aggressor keeps doing it.

Norm and Denise can't afford a maid, and Norm works two jobs, so Denise, who only works one, is stuck with the cleaning, which she hates. She has little time and little energy and doesn't get the job done to her own satisfaction. What does Norm do? He calls her "Miss White Gloves." Actually, she's not able to be "Miss White Gloves," and she feels badly about it.

Why would he use this inappropriate title? Maybe he doesn't like to see her spend so much time (in his opinion) with cleaning. Maybe he feels guilty that he isn't making enough for the maid so he's trying to demean the whole activity of cleaning. Maybe he actually thinks he's giving her a compliment that she's doing such a good job.

We will never know until he tells her in simple, inoffensive language.

Patrick is trying to take some stress out of his life. He decides to take up golf and practices a couple of times a week if he can. Naturally, his game isn't going to be that great with the limited practice time and he doesn't appreciate Marie's remark as he leaves the house, "There goes Tiger Woods."

You can guess what I'm going to say about Marie, can't you? Maybe she hates his golfing because she'd rather he spend more time with her. Maybe she doesn't like that he's not attending to household responsibilities enough. Maybe she is poor at sports herself and just doesn't understand a sports-minded person. Maybe she's nervous about who he might meet while he's on the golf links. Whatever it is, she needs to spell it out in plain words.

You can see that in all these remarks,
> They *fail* to communicate what the speaker really means
> They hurt

Just as words destroy respect, they can build it, too.

(Tool 39) Reflect on This . . .

Are you at the giving or receiving end of anything like the scenarios above? Describe the interactions.

Write a script showing how you can get your message across more directly and without pain. If you are the recipient, share this information with your partner.

Why Can't People Just Take a Joke?

Lenny thinks everything is a joke. One evening, Lenore got home a couple of hours ahead of him and made a nice roast. But she was tired. And somehow, the worst thing happened: She dropped it. Well, Lenny didn't think of himself as an abuser; he did not yell at her for dropping the roast. Instead he laughed and called her a klutz. That's name-calling.

You might be thinking, "He did not mean to be hurtful. If he's like me, he loves his wife and he doesn't want her to think he's trying to make her feel bad. It was just a joke."

In reply, let me ask you a question: Where do you draw the line? When you see a story on the news of a car accident in which someone got injured, is it funny? How about if they died?

Oh, that's where you draw the line. I see. It's only funny if it's a little thing, not a life and death matter. You might be right. So here's another question:

Where does your wife/husband draw that line? The one who was the target of your "humor"?

If your marriage partner thought it was funny, then you are right—it is funny. If not, then you lacked compassion, that ability to feel for another person. You were miles apart. The idea in a marriage is to be on the same page. Remember the reason why you got married. It was for sharing, right?

Lenore didn't think it was funny at all. She was so tired that she just broke down and cried. What did Lenny accomplish? If he thought he was lightening up the mood, he sure wasn't.

Those of you who think that these are harmless jokes might grumble, "But why does my partner have to dictate if it's funny or not? Why do I lose the power?"

The answer is: You should never have the power to afflict someone. If he doesn't think it's funny, then you're being mean—and putting yourself out of the ballpark in the relationship.

It's okay to let your partner's reaction dictate what you'll say because the next time the tables are turned and she is tempted to call you a name, she won't. She'll remember that you are decent to her.

Let's go back to Ricky's "joke" in the restaurant and take a closer look at it. Let's apply the rule that jokes are not jokes if the same "joke" made on Ricky would not make him happy. Suppose Jean said to her sister, regarding the male waiter, "Look at his tight a--." Would that be funny? Would Ricky think it was funny?

On the other hand, if Ricky and Jean were getting along great and she confessed to him in the privacy of their bedroom that she thinks men who are muscular and work out "look too full of themselves and I don't like that" and went on to point out that she thought *his* derriere was cute, then in the restaurant, he would know that she was really sending him a compliment. Now *that* would be a good joke. Only it wouldn't be on him. Or her. It would be on everyone else who wasn't in on it (and shouldn't be). So, there could be times when the joke would not be on either one of them. And that would be great, a bond between them.

Otherwise, the joke is not a joke. He was laughing *at* her. Now, you tell me, why would he do that? Here he was feeling badly, feeling rejected. Is that the way to get accepted? Is that the way to repair the damage?

Being honest means telling the difference between a joke and a dig.

> **(Tool 40) How to Tell if it's not a Joke**
> If the butt of the joke doesn't think it's funny, it's not.

Suppose the remark is accurate; it's not an exaggeration. What then?

Marge is sensitive. She cries at movies. Her husband, who feels uncomfortable with emotions, calls her a "cry-baby." He smiles when he says this, which does not automatically turn the name-calling into a joke.

Even if it's not an exaggeration but completely misses the boat in considering a person's feelings, it's still going to hurt. Maybe Marge is something of a cry-baby, but no adult would want to be called such a demeaning term.

Telling Joan that she's a "bookworm" bothers her. Maybe she realizes she's not as gifted socially as she wishes she were and this term rubs in the possibility that she escapes social situations by reading.

For the same reason, calling Sam a "backslapper" denigrates him. He's plenty gifted socially, but he hates that he says "yes" too much to people instead of telling them what he really thinks. He hasn't got the courage, and that term just rubs it in.

Benjamin couldn't stand up to his boss who reminded him of his abusive father. When his boss pushed him around, his wife called him "weak." True, it's not as bad as calling him "sissy," but, like I said, the subtle variety is just as nasty and carries the same sting.

Brutal honesty may be just plain brutal.

> **(Tool 41) One More Way to Tell if it's Name-Calling**
> If it hits too close to home, it's name-calling. Did you ever dish out or receive this sort of thing? What happened? What can you do about it now? How can you handle this in the future?

If I'm Mad at Someone, Shouldn't I Be Able to Express My Feelings So That He Knows He Did Something Wrong?

Absolutely, you should, but how is name calling an expression of your feelings? You call your husband an S.O.B, let's say. What are the feelings there?

Feelings can be expressed in one word. Examples are "angry," "depressed," "bad," and so on. You may have several feelings at one time. Right now, for example, I'm hungry, tired (it's 1 a.m.), excited (about this book's progress), and very happy (for the same reason).

Thus, the argument that you are expressing your feelings doesn't fly because calling someone a name is not such an expression. As I said previously, [Refer to pp. 61-62], name-calling actually obscures what your feelings really are.

You want power? Know what you feel!

> **(Tool 42) Reflect on This . . .**
> What am I feeling *right now*? What did I feel an hour ago? Remember, only use one word for each feeling although you may have more than one feeling at a time.

You can see from this that name-calling is not an expression of feelings. The feeling *behind* the name-calling may be anger or frustration. Fred, for example, didn't say, "I am angry at you; I am also frustrated at the situation you got us into." Now, that's an expression of feelings.

Anger destroys.

(Tool 43) Checklist: Discover Your Feelings

This exercise is important if you're angry. Anger is usually a *cover* feeling for the more vulnerable feelings like hurt and pain. Start noticing your feelings. When you're angry, take some deep breaths and, if necessary, ask, *"What kind of pain am I feeling beneath my anger?"*

Here are some possibilities:
- Feeling rejected
- Feeling neglected
- Feeling misunderstood
- Feeling disrespected
- Feeling left out
- Feeling hopeless
- Feeling depressed
- Feeling bad about myself
- Feeling ashamed of myself
- Feeling embarrassed
- Feeling stupid

Take your "feelings temperature" several times today. What did you feel?

Once you identify your feelings, you are in a much better position to know how to use them. If they're bad feelings, they're a signal to take care of yourself, just like a burn means "get away from that heat" or internal aches serve as a signal that it's time to see your doctor. If they're good feelings, then, enjoy them! Knowing what you feel is a major step in taking care of yourself. In your relationship, it means better communication, less fighting, and ultimately, wonderful intimacy.

Keep a log of the feelings you have from the checklist above (Tool 43).

Can you feel the power when you recognize a pattern?

(Tool 44) Reflect on This . . .

Did you see any patterns in your feelings? What did you learn about yourself?

Next, I want to look at one example of name-calling that comes up often.

Chapter Six
"My Partner is Hypersensitive"

When Lenny told Lenore she was a klutz, she started to cry. Lenny couldn't understand this. If someone told him he was a klutz, he'd say they were right and let it go. He shrugged his shoulders and walked off muttering, "Boy, is she hypersensitive," thus compounding his mistake.

When one person calls another, "hypersensitive," it's name-calling. There may be good reasons why a label like "klutz" would not hurt Lenny. The fact that calling Lenore a klutz does hurt his wife does not make her hypersensitive. Also, we showed in Chapter Five that if the label is accurate, it can hurt all the more [Refer to pp. 65-66]. So if she is a klutz, calling her one will really sting.

Lenny didn't stop at calling Lenore a klutz. He also called her "hypersensitive." Why is that wrong? Let's start examining this by looking at why Lenny isn't too easily bothered by name-calling."

Although Lenny doesn't recall much from his childhood—a typical reaction to a painful one—he distinctly remembers one trip to the mall. He was really happy that day. At five, the world is so interesting. He was looking in the windows of the shops and suddenly he realized his mother was angry at him. "Come on," she said, "What's wrong with you anyway?"

Of course, nothing was wrong with him—until that moment. He had no idea what he could have done wrong. Being five, he started to sniffle. "Cry baby," his mother said. He remembers that second because it was the day he finally decided there was no point in listening to his mother. She had nothing good to say.

He got mistreated and toughened up from it. He became numb to his own bad feelings. The process occurs as a brilliant coping mechanism of the human soul. If Lenny were aware of his pain (as some people, indeed, are) he would be suffering constantly. He was just a little kid. So he got numb. Or he dissociated. Numbness is a kind of dissociation.[1] It's a way of being here yet the emotional part of him has taken a hike.

This can happen to boys who were told not to feel, or "Be a man!" But it happens to women, too.

Ironically, Lenny ended up becoming programmed. His mom would make fun of his feelings, so subconsciously, he decided she must be right and having feelings must be wrong. He stopped having any. He didn't *think* he was doing it to be obedient. He probably thought he was in rebellion. He thought that by not feeling and saying "I don't care" when they scolded him, that was rebellion. Instead, he was programmed not to feel the pain they dished out, and it worked.

This suited Lenny's parents because now they didn't have to watch their language. They could keep dishing it out, and Lenny wouldn't feel it. Instead of correcting their damaging approach, they could make *him* be the "bad guy." Pretty clever. And of course, he was a little kid, so he bought it. And he didn't know he bought it.

That approach backfires. When the child gets older, parents wonder why their so-called discipline didn't "work." Lenny was out of control. Nothing they said "got through" to him. Well, of course. He "didn't care." That was due to their programming.

Here's another story:

Jason's father was involved in his work. Greatly involved. He got real satisfaction from work, and, unfortunately, his relationship with his wife had gotten stale. Instead of doing anything about it, he spent long hours at the office. Jason's mother felt that chill. It made her unhappy and she turned inward. She prided herself on performing her responsibilities as a mom: She always had dinner on the table; the clothes were cleaned and put away; the house was neat; they had the obligatory holiday dinners and family visits. All that made the house look like a home was there. But in actuality, it wasn't a home. Jason could not get an emotional response from his father. When he asked his dad for advice, he was brushed off with, "You're big enough to know that." When he asked his dad for participation, his dad was too busy. He yearned for his dad—and got nothing.

His mom, in pain, didn't reach out to him, either. He didn't yearn for her, anyway; a boy wants a father to emulate. She busied herself with her responsibilities in an automatic way. To Jason, she was a shadow.

About the age of thirteen, he discovered that there were other boys like him online. He reached out to them. He wasn't so lonely any more. His parents were glad he seemed so self-sufficient; they didn't want to be bothered and he didn't bother them any more. The online gang was into finding out how to build bombs, and he thought that was fun. The idea of shaking up people (translate "parents") who could not be shaken up was a thrill. Jason learned, much to his delight, that when he got to high school, one or two of the online chums were there in the flesh. It wasn't long before the group of them got in trouble. When the police interviewed his parents, Jason's parents were stupefied. The investigators found nothing abnormal in the home either. That is because no overt abuse was present. There was plenty of emotional neglect, but investigators would have a hard time seeing that.

It only takes a small amount of emotional neglect from parents to create a totally insensitive person, so insensitive that he is not even deterred from acts of violence. Will every neglected child become violent? Of course not, but trying to guess which one will and which one won't is like playing Russian Roulette.

If it doesn't take much of this "ordinary" insensitivity on parents' part to create a violent person, then that same "ordinary" insensitivity will most likely create another insensitive person.

Research bears me out. Osofsky and Osofsky, professors of psychiatry, claim: "Children who are victimized are at much higher risk of becoming either victims or perpetrators themselves."[2] They do not mention violence: Children who are victimized are at risk of becoming insensitive, if not violent, adults.

What's your sensitivity level?

(Tool 45) Reflect on This . . .

Are you insensitive? Were you abused or neglected growing up? Did that increase or decrease your sensitivity?

Eventually, Lenny may understand that it is not so much that Lenore is hypersensitive, but that he might be insensitive. As an insensitive person, Lenny is not getting all the information that his senses are trying to give him; he's missing out!

When Lenny reaches adulthood, he is numb and well prepared for the nastiness in the world—because he doesn't feel pain! He can fight like a bear at work and come out on top. Or be a politician. (Ever wonder how they can take the mud that others sling at them? Well, that could be one answer.) But along comes Lenore who says, "You hurt me." Now, he's puzzled. His logical thought is: "She must be hypersensitive." Actually, no. She's normal. What happened is he didn't know that he got desensitized. When he knows it, he's going to remember the pain that led to it—and then he's no longer desensitized.

If he wants to remain tough for the rough and tumble of business or politics, he won't want to change. A little insensitivity will act like Novocaine on a drilled tooth. On the other hand, if he wants to respect Lenore's feelings, he will have to learn what makes her feel so badly. And then he'll have to decide how sensitive he wants to get. Because the more sensitive he is, the harder that tooth drilling—the world of business or politics or his relations with his parents—will be to take.

Lenore is unhappy because Lenny is insensitive, but as he grows in sensitivity, they will both lead happier, richer lives. You see, a sensitive person not only feels more pain but is quite capable of feeling greater levels of joy. A numb person, on the other hand, doesn't feel much joy. He's numb, after all.

The meaning of the word sensitive is not "easily hurt." It means being able to feel and sense what's going on. Now, that may end up meaning the person *does* get hurt. Because if you can feel your feelings and you know someone hurt them, then you should get hurt. That's exactly how we were made to function. Otherwise, why else were we given feelings?

Nevertheless, the more sensitive the person, the more empowered the person is. Being sensitive would be like being a great vocalist with perfect pitch. She can hear the difference between being slightly off key or on.

Taking pride in your softer side is empowering.

(Tool 46) Reflect on This . . .
Have you been called hypersensitive? Do you think that's true? If not, what do you think is the truth?

Sensitivity vs. Victim Thinking
➤ Victim thinking is feeling hurt when absolutely nothing was done to injure you. Victim thinking is self-destructive.
➤ Sensitivity means feeling wounded when something *was* done to injure you. Sensitivity is normal and appropriate.
➤ Verbal aggression should hurt.

Normal people feel pain. If they are attacked, they should feel it. If they don't, it means they are insensitive.

There is no such thing as hypersensitivity. Either you are numb or you are sensitive.

Let's look at some instances and see whether they are examples of victim thinking or appropriate sensitivity.

1. *Jason marries Sue. He forgets their anniversary. She's hurt.* Is that playing victim or being appropriately sensitive?

An anniversary means that the day you married is a day to be cherished, a landmark in your lives. To forget it is to nullify it. For this reason, Sue has every reason to expect their anniversary to be remembered and she is being appropriately sensitive.

Now, you may wonder how to handle it if you find yourself approaching an anniversary and you and your partner have been fighting so you don't feel so close and loving right now. Here's my advice: If you are reading this book, it means you want things to be better. So get the flowers and the card anyway. Tell her that although right now things are strained, you still care.

2. *Steve tells Marcia her cooking is terrible. She's hurt.* Is that victim thinking or being appropriately sensitive?

Taste is a personal thing. Steve is thinking that he is the official taste tester. He's not. If he doesn't care for his wife's cooking, he should politely suggest she make dishes he prefers. He could cook with her, too, as long as it's a fun experience and not one of criticism. His approach was unkind and Marcia is not being oversensitive at all.

3. *Steve doesn't eat dinner. He excuses himself glumly and goes to his room. Marcia thinks he doesn't like her food.* Is that victim thinking or being sensitive?

While it is true that Steve has said her cooking was terrible, each new situation is different. Marcia is required to give her husband the benefit of the doubt each and every time. Perhaps he was disturbed about something at work. Perhaps Steve had eaten a large lunch. Perhaps he has work to do tonight and it's on his mind. Perhaps he is, indeed, upset with Marcia and would rather take a time out than have a fight or hurt her feelings. These are all examples of how to give the benefit of the doubt. Jumping to a conclusion in the absence of solid proof is victim thinking on Marcia's part.

I'd like you to note something important here: In Example 2, Marcia is being victimized. Yet, because she is not being victimized in Example 3, she has the difficult and challenging task of not automatically falling into that victim role with regard to her husband. Even though she is—perhaps often—a victim, she can't allow herself to mechanically think like one. She must take each case anew. If she does not do this, she will become depressed, even hopeless. In each new instance, she must try to give the benefit of the doubt.

To play Devil's advocate, I also caution that Marcia must look carefully at each new instance. That means she cannot automatically assume that Steve is *not* trying to hurt her, either. Overlooking one's own victimization is not self-protective and not wise.

4. *Warren calls Kathy names. She's hurt.* Is that victim thinking or being appropriately sensitive?

By now, you know that name-calling is verbal abuse. It is healthy and normal to be hurt by it and therefore Kathy's reaction is appropriate.

5. *Warren tells Kathy he's tired. She decides that means he doesn't want to spend time with her and feels hurt.* Is that victim thinking or being sensitive?

Even though Warren has been hurtful in the past, each case must be taken on its own. If Warren claims to be tired, any other conclusion is victim thinking on Kathy's part.

Increasing sensitivity and decreasing victim thinking will heal you.

(Tool 47) Reflect on This . . .
Go over every incident of the last two weeks in which either
you or your partner felt hurt. Decide for each whether it was
appropriate sensitivity or victim thinking.

Jean and Ricky

Frequently, an insensitive person will know deep inside that something in
her is missing and will search for a sensitive person to marry.

Suppose Jean was a really, really sensitive lady. When she was painting
the living room baby blue and her husband walked in and didn't say
anything, she could tell the difference between his being angry and cold
versus being hurt. That would be sensitive. Then she'd know that he was
hurt and she'd know it was because she went ahead with the paint job
without consulting him. Her sensitivity would be a huge asset.

Sensitivity is being able to read a person. If Ricky had come in growling,
that's one thing. But he didn't. He kind of had a hang-dog look as he came
in. His shoulders were slumped a little. He kind of shuffled to his room.
He didn't slam the door. He wasn't loud. That would show anger. Instead,
he was quiet and withdrawn. You could call that "cold." It sure seemed
like it, but it would be a wrong reading.

So how would Jean know? The best way is to begin by giving Ricky the
benefit of the doubt. When in doubt, assume the other person's mood is
not a hostile or negative one. The therapist picked it up right away if you
remember from the scenario. She asked Ricky if he went to his room to
sulk and he admitted to it.

A cold person may have contact with other people. A cold person may
address the person she is giving the cold shoulder to in a superior way.

A cold person is frequently trying to make a point, and therefore, is functioning just fine otherwise. But when a person is sulking, the sulk permeates the whole mood.

If Jean were a sensitive person, she'd have immediately realized that she had hurt Ricky. Let's see how that scene would have been different:

Jean [to herself]: Uh-oh. I blew it. I'm in trouble now. He's hurt. Dang.

Jean [to Ricky]: You're hurt. I can tell. Look, I'm sorry. I didn't think the paint job mattered to you, or I would have tried harder to get your opinion on it. I really didn't mean to leave you out.

Ricky: Well, you did. And it wasn't nice.

Jean: I tried to talk to you, but you kept avoiding me. I don't know why you've been avoiding me. Why have you?

Pause action. She is sensitive, but she is not a mind reader. Important distinction. If you remember, he felt hurt that she wouldn't have sex with him after Goldie, their baby, arrived. She didn't realize that. He never told her. She figured he just didn't know how to be helpful and wasn't a helpful individual. This conclusion does not fit with the rule that it is better to give the person the benefit of the doubt. Jean can deduce some things but not others. She may be right that he doesn't know how to help. She may be right that he is jealous of Goldie, the baby. But where she misses the boat is assuming that the jealousy comes from his being selfish rather than that he simply does not understand what it's like to have a baby. And the sex part is totally beyond her comprehension. But now that she opened the door to a real conversation *because her sensitivity was able to pick up what the real problem was*, he's ready and willing to answer the question. So, to continue the dialogue—

Ricky: You know why.

[Jean has a totally baffled look on her face. Ricky is not a sensitive person. He does not see the difference between being baffled and playing games with him.]

Jean: No, I don't. Why?

[Ricky believes she is playing games. He also wants this to work. Therefore, he takes the plunge and acts as if he is giving her the benefit of the doubt and that she really doesn't know what he is talking about.]

Ricky: You avoided sex. Now, are you happy I said it?

[Jean's jaw drops open].

Jean: Are you for real?

[Now it's Ricky's turn to be surprised. He was sure she was playing games. But here she really is surprised. It begins to seem like she is sincere.]

Ricky: Of course. [He stares at her.]

Because Jean is a pretty sensitive person, she sees that he really is confused. He is surprised at her surprise! This opens up the door to real conversation. She has to explain to him her tiredness after birth and her disappointment at his not helping with the baby. She is tired and drained even now as they speak. But her sensitivity oils the wheels of that conversation.

So the bottom line is this: There's no such thing as being too sensitive. If someone is easily hurt because someone hurt them, they *should* be hurt. Is it normal to break your bone and not hurt? Of course not.

Sensitivity for others defeats victim thinking.

(Tool 48) Reflect on this . . .

If you consider yourself sensitive, are you more sensitive to your own feelings or other people's feelings? Give some examples. Which way do you want to be?

Control

What does this all have to do with control? Being sensitive, aware, and tuned in is tantamount to being alive. Yet, interestingly enough, it is also a basis for name-calling. What is really happening when your partner tells you that you are hypersensitive is she wants to be able to continue to dish out the remarks. Prior to reading this book, your partner didn't want to do the work of changing behavior.

As soon as you call it like it is—abuse—and you declare the right to feel hurt, your partner loses the ability to control you.

How to Stop the Hypersensitivity Nonsense

Now, I'm really going to empower you. The next time you are called hypersensitive, shoot back, "You are saying that because you are insensitive. That's a shame. You're missing a lot." Grin if you can. Don't say anything more.

If you can't muster up a grin, it is perfectly okay to say this while you are crying. If the aggressor injured you and you cry, so be it; but in the meantime, let him know the truth. When you do this, your name-caller loses control over the right to decide how much he can mistreat you.

Assertive responses, well-delivered, are empowering.

**(Tool 49) How to Stop this Particular
Name-Calling**

Tell him, "You are insensitive. That's a shame. You're missing a lot."

Chapter Seven
Put-downs: They're No Joke

Bob worked hard on the dinner. He was out of work and already felt badly about that. His wife worked so hard, and he wanted to at least do something nice. He put some time into finding a recipe in the cookbook, getting fresh ingredients, and making it. At dinner, Marla commented, "Give up. Cooking's not your thing."

Do you notice how you don't need to use nasty language in order to hurt someone? What's more, Marla's comment is a put-down, another version of name-calling. Perhaps it seems innocent, just a candid remark. But it's not.

If you have difficulty seeing this remark for what it is, you may be like the people who have red-green color blindness. They think the world is "normal" the way they see it. They not only don't know what they're missing, it's impossible to convey it to them. Growing up in a damaging home is like that. It seems so normal that those involved don't even realize that what has been dished out may have been very cruel.

"Sticks and stones" are not the only things that can damage. Knowing what put-downs really are, the damage they do to the soul, how they escalate, and how to respond to them will erase the myth that "words can never harm me."

What Put-Downs Aren't

Put-downs are not "harmless jokes." The test of the difference between a put-down and a joke, as discussed in Tool 40 of Chapter Five, Name-Calling Is No Big Deal--Or Is It [Refer to p. 65] was whether the receiver thinks it's funny. If he doesn't, it's not.

But another test is: Would the *jokester* be happy if someone he respected used that very same so-called joke on him? This question may or may not work. People who claim to be only making a joke could say it wouldn't bother them if that joke were on them as Lenny did in Chapter Six, My Partner is Hypersensitive. Others, more honest, or more sensitive, will have an "aha" experience when this tool is employed.

Restore respect by working at recognizing the pain in your jokes.

**(Tool 50) Another Way to Tell if it's Name-Calling,
a Put-down, or just a Harmless Joke**
How would the jokester like it if the tables were turned?

Put-downs are also not "constructive criticism." At a construction site, people are building something. To give the kind of criticism that is constructive, you must see evidence of it helping the receiver to grow. For instance, when my children were little, they took violin lessons. When they hit a wrong note after having practiced long and hard, the teacher would say, "I can tell you have been practicing well." She would then recite, very specifically, five or so things they did well. Then—and only then—she would say, "Now play that [name of note] again for me." If it was right this time, she would say, "Do you hear the difference from before?" This helped the child feel good about what was done right and turned the mistake into an opportunity to train the ear.

In contrast, "You played the wrong note!" is just plain criticism, not constructive. And, "You played the wrong note again. I don't know what's the matter with you" is a put-down guaranteed to make the child hate music *and* it will ruin your relationship.

Enjoy the power of constructive criticism.

(Tool 51) How to Give Constructive Criticism
1. Compliment—sincerely—what the person did *right*.
2. Ask a *thinking question* that the person should be able to answer about the error.
3. Compliment the correct answer to that question.

Put-downs are also not the best way to express exasperation with those you love. What is heard is rejection. The responses could be: to reciprocate that rejection, to feel depressed over that kind of treatment, or to get out of the relationship.

Put-downs are anything that attacks the other person or what that person holds dear. They can be as subtle as eyeball rolling or a cold tone of voice. They can be as obvious as cursing. They can be things in between, such as referring to your son's friends as, "Oh, those people," and your husband's skill at softball as, "It was great thirty years ago." The best way to know if you have put someone down is to ask yourself honestly what your feelings really are about the person to whom it was directed.

The best way to know if you have been put down is to ask yourself if you feel proud after hearing that remark.

Self-empowerment is being able to look yourself in the mirror.

(Tool 52) Reflect on This . . .
Notice your feelings next time you put down someone you love. Do you feel more like you *got even* for something, or do you feel simply happy? What do you suppose you got even for? Were you unhappy before you made the remark? Can you admit that what you said really was a put-down?

Recipients of put-downs must stop sweeping the dust under the rug in order to keep "peace." Your empowerment comes when you recognize that you have been mistreated.

> **(Tool 53) Reflect on This…**
> For recipients, how do put-downs make *you* feel? Does it undermine your sense of self?

Mike and Laura got into it again. "You think you're so smart!" Laura screamed. "Well you're not!"

Both her first comment and her second are put-downs.

"So how much money did you make today?" asked Phil of Sal.

Sometimes the only way to know if a put-down occurred is from the context. Phil knew that Sal didn't spend as many hours working today as she wanted or needed to because she took her mother to a doctor's appointment. Phil objected to her spending her time on her mother who didn't really like him and let him know it. To convey his feelings, he threw in her face her poor earnings. As you can see, he didn't convey his feelings at all. What it accomplished is that it hurt his wife.

Marjorie had trouble losing weight. She decided to buy herself something new to cheer herself up. But when Al saw her in it, he said, "Sorry, dear, you don't make the grade."

Interesting, isn't it, that even with the "sorry" and the "dear" you can't get away from a put down?

And the so-called joke: After Marjorie started to cry, Al said, "Okay, okay, you look adorable."

Jamal surveyed the work still piled up on Shenika's desk. "Boy, you really are slow," he commented.

Tune into your feelings.

(Tool 54) Reflect on This . . .

Is it possible that some of the "innocent" remarks you make are really put-downs?

Is it possible that the reason you feel really awful after some of your conversations is because you got put down and didn't realize it?

The Damage Put-Downs Do to the Soul

Unfortunately, unlike a courtroom in which the judge can instruct the jury to "please disregard that," once said, a put-down enters the soul in much the same way a virus enters a cell: destructively. Each and every time a put-down is leveled at someone, the soul is injured badly. Health professionals see the manifestation of this daily.[1]

People who hear put-downs often enough begin to doubt themselves. They begin to think there must indeed be something wrong with them or those they love wouldn't be so mean. They go beyond thinking there is some aspect of themselves that is wrong; rather, they think their whole selves are wrong. God, somehow, mis-made them.

No matter how angry you are with someone, you don't want to do this. You may think you do, but when you act out of anger, the damage boomerangs: Doing it injures *your* soul, too. And you can easily tell that it has. You somehow don't feel happy afterward; you are not relieved or unburdened. Rather, you feel as miserable and perhaps as angry as you did before.

Giving up a momentary high yields a long-term benefit.

(Tool 55) Reflect on This . . .
How do you feel after you've put someone down? Do you
really feel better? How long does that "better" feeling last?
Does it lead to your getting what you want? How does it
affect your relationship?

How They Escalate: Back to Ricky and Jean

Let's see how put-downs can make bad problems worse. Let's assume that
the sensitivity that Jean had in Chapter Six did not occur. What follows is
a continuation of Chapter One:

*After they got home from their interview with the counselor, Jean was
angry. She was angry at herself for having cried; she was angry at Ricky
for putting her in this embarrassing situation; she was angry at life for
giving her a bad lot. And she was tired. Being tired after a baby comes is
normal, and having your emotions get the best of you when you are tired
is normal, too.*

*Jean was furious with Ricky, and she told him off. Thinking of all the
nights she got up alone to attend to Goldie and his crazy demands for sex
after Goldie was born, she called him a "selfish, lazy bum." She saw the
dagger enter his heart. She saw the look on his face. He was quiet and
there was a moment of peace. But in that moment, Jean did not feel relief.
How can she?*

*It did not undo the damage that Ricky already did. Nor did she give him a
chance to apologize or make it good. Nothing was corrected. Jean thought
she got even, but what her heart craves is love, attention, assistance,
companionship, and acceptance—and she sure didn't set up the situation
for that. Ricky, meanwhile, didn't have the foggiest idea of what he could
do about it at this point. He didn't understand before; he sure didn't now.*

But he was really angry himself now, and who knows where that will lead?

Ricky and Jean are alienated, angry, miserable, and depressed. The put-down did not convey emotions; it stirred up worse emotions.

Did you notice how Jean, the "victim," turned into the aggressor? See what self-justification accomplishes?

How to Respond

If someone puts you down, first you have to recognize it for what it is. Once you do, here are four possible types of responses:

1. *Name it*. That way you give the down-putter the benefit of the doubt. Maybe she didn't realize that it was a put-down. Maybe she just thought it was a joke or constructive criticism. Maybe she just thought, "Well, that's what I do to vent anger," without meaning to put down. The solution here is tell it like it is and say, "That was a put down."

The minute he walked into his living room and saw the baby blue walls, Ricky could have said, "I can't believe you didn't ask me what color I would like. I feel totally put down in this relationship."

Or, when Ricky made the crack at the restaurant, instead of crying and running out, Jean could have said, "How could you put me down like that!"

Notice something very important in the Jean/Ricky thing: The putting down process is really subtle. Ricky being left out of the paint decision *was* a put-down. It amounted to saying, "He's not important." It wasn't said in words, but the meaning was there, and that's the meaning he got—even though she didn't even mean it!

Jean was licking her own wounds. When you are preoccupied with yourself and your own feelings, that's the moment you could be unkind

89

to another person. She didn't paint the living room to annoy him, just to comfort herself. But in the process, she knew she left him out. She didn't mean to be cruel to him, but she definitely knew she had left him out. And that made him feel bad.

And the same thing could be said for Ricky. His remark over the waitress's anatomy could be taken as a fact. Maybe the waitress was attractive; just a fact, ma'am. But what a fact! It's a fact that puts her, his wife to whom his soul is joined, beneath a total stranger, a put-down if there ever was one.

2. *Throw the ball back to his court.* Ask, "Did you really want to say it that way, because it was a put down?" A reflective person might think about it and realize that she didn't intend that and make some correction or apology right on the spot. Jean certainly would get some applause from the audience had she composed herself and said this to Ricky at the restaurant.

3. *Say it hurt.* This suggestion comes with a warning: Only do it with a person of good will. If the person who said it is so angry that he just wants to inflict wounds, saying it felt bad can, unfortunately, lead to more of the same. For other people, saying the put-down hurt can, indeed, put a stop to it. Had Ricky just walked into that living room and announced that seeing the paint job in process without him made him feel bad, I'll bet that relationship would have been patched up very quickly.

Men, I'll give you a hint here: Letting women know your soft side is a big strength. Women go wild for sensitive men. It brings down their own tough exterior very quickly, too. After all, they only put that on as a defense against the mean things you have said. Stop being mean, recognize your own feelings, and let her know what they are.

4. *Challenge.* When the sender of the message honestly cannot see that the message is highly critical and not constructive at all, challenging the statement on a purely logical basis can be a wonderful experience in empowerment. (Of course, you have to calm down first. Such discussions

cannot take place when one or the other is still fuming.)

However, being logical isn't enough. Not only do you have to say that the other person's statement was wrong, critical, and not constructive, you have to say it was hurtful—when that's a safe thing to do. See, even though we're trying to be logical, you always have to bring the subject back to feelings. If you don't, that other person will not understand how very damaging the remarks are.

Let's go back to the restaurant. Let's rewrite it.

Jean does stand up to Ricky. With her nose in the air and a sniff, she says, "You put me down," (Number 1, naming it) "and, besides that, it was hurtful." (Number 3, saying it hurt).

However, since he felt hurt because of the paint project, Ricky didn't really care about her feelings. Nevertheless, he loves her and does not want to injure her, so, in front of everyone, he declares, "Well, how do you think I felt when I walked in and found you painting without telling me anything about it?" (Number 4, challenge)

Now, they're having—drum roll, please—a conversation. A conversation about important things. Finally. With that conversation started, I can guarantee you that Jean and Ricky did not have a fight that ended in the middle of the night.

Incidentally, one reviewer of this book questioned my rewrite, above. She thought that Ricky should apologize for hurting Jean's feelings before telling her that his feelings were hurt. In an ideal world, she's right. He should. But I've found that most people are so intent on dealing with their own hurt feelings, they can't make that big a step. So, I'm okay with him at least expressing his own feelings first. At least, he's dealing with real feelings and not the anger that covers them up. Hopefully, in the middle of this discussion, the appropriate apologies will come.

Confront abuse directly, calmly, and without counterattack and you will feel fantastic.

(Tool 56) How to Handle Put-downs

1. Name it.
2. Ask if she really wanted to say it that way.
3. Say it hurt.
4. Challenge the actual put-down.

Which do you do? Does it work? What else could you try?

Chapter Eight
Blame Boomerangs

The children were grown and gone. You'd think that Jack and Shelly would enjoy their empty nest, but no such luck. Their oldest, Aaron, was 32 and not yet married. "If you hadn't given in to his every whim," Jack said, "he wouldn't be so spoiled. He'd be satisfied with a nice girl." "I did not spoil him," retorted Shelly weakly.

As if a discussion now about what happened three decades ago would make a difference. Is this the way to find happiness?

And when I confront blamers, they tell me that they love their partner. So what gives? What in the world do you love about them if they are responsible for every problem you have? If you think I'm implying that maybe they didn't even deserve the blame in the first place, you're right. Sometimes it's a matter of being in the *habit* of blaming someone when it absolutely wasn't deserved.

Couples will raise the question with me, "Well, DrDeb, what if they really did upset me and I don't tell them? Won't they keep on doing the same thing?" The problem is that if you *do* keep piling blame and accusation on them, I *guarantee* they'll keep doing it. After all, you're making them feel miserable, so what is their motivation to be nice to you?

Ever hear the old expression, "You get more flies with honey than with vinegar?" Your relationship will fall apart, if it hasn't already, if you feel a need to point a finger over everything that goes wrong. You can't rewrite the past by rehashing it, and you definitely don't create what those in the business world call "good will." What's more, constant blame, over the lifetime of a marriage is traumatic.

So put the brakes on that behavior. Pronto.

"Wait a minute, DrDeb," you're probably thinking, "how *do* I let my partner know that he is doing something wrong if I don't say anything?"

And my answer is: There's a right way to do it and a wrong way. The way that sounds like blame and accusation does not work. It backfires badly.

How Did You Start the Blaming Thing, Anyway?

It started one of three ways:
- ➢ One: Your parents did it to each other and to you.
- ➢ Two: As a little kid, you discovered that when you blamed someone else, you got away with things.
- ➢ Three: You don't know how else to rid yourself of the uncomfortable feeling that you're left with when something goes wrong.

Let's take these one by one.

<u>One</u>: Your parents did it to each other and to you.
We learn from watching our parents. We assume something is normal because that's what we see. I remember someone telling me that she thought her house without a dining room table, without dinners together, without conversation, but with hostility and anger, was normal. That is, until she got to high school and was in other people's homes. Her parents did what many abusive families did; they tried for years, all her growing up years, to prevent her from finding out that this was *not* normal. So they wouldn't allow her to go visit friends.

But you know how teenagers are—thank God. They are independent and inquisitive and they reach out to their friends for support if they're not getting it at home. So this woman found out the truth: Blaming is *not* normal. I say "thank God" because going to friends' homes gave her an opportunity to learn for the first time how to be a human being, how to relate without the blaming. But until you really see it, feel it, hear how the sentences play out, you don't know how else to deal with problems when you've never had a non-blaming family.

Here's a test to see if your parents' way of relating is heavy on blame: If it *feels awful* to relate to them most of the time, then something is seriously wrong. If you are an adult and you find that most of your adult relationships are just like the one you had with your parents growing up and *those* relationships feel awful, then you have probably unwittingly duplicated those kinds of bad relationships among your friends, with your partner, and possibly with your own children, as well. You may be the blamer or the blamed; either way, it doesn't feel good—and something needs fixing.

Life shouldn't feel awful. Relationships shouldn't be painful. Life should be a joy, and when stressful circumstances happen, well, that's life. But it is not an excuse to blame someone else for not handling things right, even if your parents did that.

Rooting out unhealthy ways of relating is liberating.

(Tool 57) Reflect on This . . .

If your relationship with your parents feels awful, it may have been poisoned by blame. Ditto other relationships. Have you noticed overt or implicit blame? Describe instances. Write verbatim what you and others have said that just doesn't feel good.

Ricky's case fits here to a "t". When Ricky's father walked out, Ricky felt—as so many, many children do—that it was his fault. Why do these children feel that way? Where does such a wild idea come from? The answer is, in one word, blame. If the child has already been used to being blamed a good deal of the time, he automatically thinks, "This, too, is my fault." It is an assumption he makes. And the assumption makes perfect sense when you figure the history of blame in a given family.

In Ricky's family, we don't know that he was explicitly blamed for his father's abandonment of the family, but his mother never said anything to change his assumption of self-blame. How many parents sit down with their child and explicitly say, "It was NOT your fault"? About anything, not just about a divorce. Anything.

I once knew a child who grew up severely depressed because a brother had died in a freak accident. Why did that child grow up depressed when she was nowhere near the scene of the accident and had nothing to do with it? Simply because the parents' overwhelming grief and depression over the loss of the other sibling made the child who still lived feel worthless. She said more than once, "I should have died instead. They don't love me anyway." Here, no blame was spoken, but the little child mistakenly took her parents' grief for blame. And they never said, "We love you so much. Thank God you're still with us!" Without that, she never believed that that was the truth. Silence can be toxic.

The rule then, in addition to not blaming the other person, is to make a point of verbally refuting any possible misconceptions the individual has that she is being blamed.

Clearing self-blame is as good as throwing out rotten tomatoes.

> **(Tool 58) Reflect on This . . .**
> When bad things happened, were you told—explicitly—it was NOT your fault? What assumptions did you make about whose fault it was?

<u>Two</u>: Somebody's got to be at fault.
Maybe your parents didn't blame you or each other, but somehow, as a child, you got in the bad habit of blaming your brother or sister. This happens in families where the children have cleverly learned that they can get out of punishments by pointing a finger at someone else. The parents don't realize that they are encouraging irresponsibility and a bad attitude this way. Now you grew up with the ridiculous idea that just by blaming someone, the problem will go away.

If you look at all the terrible mistakes in life, there is, indeed, plenty of fault to go around. But, so what? Finding out who is at fault does not solve or even reduce the problem. Have you found that it does?

No longer blaming others is a giant step towards rebuilding trust.

> **(Tool 59) Reflect on This . . .**
> Can you imagine not looking for someone to blame for problems? How would you manage?

Three: You don't know what to do with your bad feelings.
Finally, a big reason people blame is the same as the reason they get angry: to get rid of those uncomfortable feelings they're left with when confronted with some problem. Like, "What do I do now?" Actually, nothing. "But, but, but . . .I *can't* just sit here and not say anything about this awful situation!" Yeah, you can. See, letting it go is very hard. But that is part of life. Just let it go. Once it has happened, there is no way you can undo it and certainly not by pinning the blame on someone.

Now I'm going to tell you why it is in your best interest to stop blaming.

Why Blaming Boomerangs

Blaming guarantees the problem will come back. Why? For several reasons:

1. The person who got blamed is not going to listen to blame. So he shuts down. Therefore, nothing is learned or gained from the blaming episode.

This is clear from Jean and Ricky's story. Both felt blamed by the other and both shut down. Jean felt blamed for not being attentive enough to Ricky after Goldie arrived, and Ricky felt blamed for not helping with her.

Some of that was victim thinking and some of that was real blame. Let's examine the difference:

Victim thinking is *assuming* the other person is blaming you. It comes from having been blamed as a child by your parents, or currently by your partner.

Blaming, on the other hand, is real. It's when someone actually says something to the other person.

When Goldie arrived, Jean was tired, wanted help with her, and Ricky didn't help. All he wanted was sex. When the counselor asked Jean why Ricky didn't help, Jean said, "Maybe he is just plain selfish." That's blame.

She needed to give him the benefit of the doubt instead. Remember, before Goldie came, she didn't see him in this bad light. By labeling him, even if only to herself, she is not opening up a door for a healthy conversation.

On his part, Ricky suffered from victim thinking and then, as a consequence, he did some blaming of his own. He assumed his wife was rejecting him when she was just tired. Based on a faulty assumption, he attacked back instead of giving her the benefit of the doubt.

You see the way blame shuts everyone down? Ricky neglected Jean after Goldie came, so she paid him back by unilaterally deciding to paint the room.

2. Furthermore, just to make matters worse, the blamer loses good will with the person she is attacking.

Good will is that intangible thing that allows people to make a mistake once in a while. It's like when a store has a really good return policy, you want to shop there more. The store has to cover the added expense of all those returns, but their good will pays off handsomely when their customers come back for repeat business.

It's the same with couples. If the one who feels justified to blame doesn't go ahead with the blame, then when that person screws up, the person who didn't get blamed feels charitable and says, "Oh, well; we're all human; don't worry about it."

Even when the blame is justified, don't do it. Don't let your head get into a negative mindset about your partner.

If you want empowerment in your relationships, this tool is a treasure.

> **(Tool 60) Explain This . . .**
> In your own words, explain good will.

But when you're into blaming, forget it; you have not created the good will. Without good will, why should the person you blamed care if he messes you up in the future? You can see how this boomerangs.

If Ricky had said, "I really miss your attention, but you must be tired a lot from the baby"—and then helped her, *even if he didn't believe that was the truth*—he would have acquired goodwill. Jean would have appreciated his help; the relationship would have been friendly, and although she still wouldn't have wanted sex for a while, she sure wouldn't have gone and painted that room without him. Of course, if he actually believed her, so much the better.

They would have muddled through until she felt better, and then, because of the stored-up good will he had obtained, one day would have wanted sex with him. Acting as if he gave her the benefit of the doubt—good will—would have made the wait worthwhile.

That's what couples do who don't get into the victim thinking-and-blame rut. They either give the benefit of the doubt and believe their partner's good intentions or they act as if they did.

Expanding this one valuable tool to two is even more powerful.

(Tool 61) Explain This . . .

Explain his two choices in using good will and how that would have gotten them over this bad period.

---

3. The person who is being blamed loses faith in herself. If you can't do anything right, you start to not know what is right. If you are always wrong, you're going to be mentally distracted, sad, lacking in concentration, confused, unsure.

Anything bad in life can have this effect. Would you be surprised to hear that the number of people in car accidents following a diagnosis of a loved one with cancer is higher than in the general population? That's because the person can't think. The problem has taken over.

The same logic applies when you are always wrong, i.e., blamed. You start to believe it. You become confused, unclear, unsure. And then, by a funny "coincidence," the blamed one really does screw up, which "proves" that the blamer was right. Of course, it doesn't prove anything of the sort. What really happened is that the blamer caused the very problem he didn't want just by blaming.

Am I saying that being constantly blamed over the lifetime of a marriage is as painful to a person as losing a beloved partner? Yes, actually I am. It's as painful and it can lead to the same level of self-doubt, confusion, depression, and lack of identity as losing a beloved partner. That is why strained marriages will have a higher incidence of health complaints than the general population.[1] The confusion, depression and other emotional symptoms take their toll on the body.

Blame is toxic; keep it out of your life.

(Tool 62) Explain This . . .
Explain why someone who is constantly blamed performs poorly.

Both Jean and Ricky suffered from being blamed. Jean just had a baby, yet she went back to work *and* managed the house. She did so much, yet it wasn't enough. Ricky's coldness made her feel totally demoralized. No wonder she was depressed, confused, and in need of a pick-me-up. Remember, that's why she started the painting project. Ricky's implicit blame made Jean feel that she could do nothing, absolutely nothing, to make things better with him.

Ricky ended up in the exact same boat. He interpreted her fatigue as coldness, but eventually his coldness and neglect led her to *be* cold and neglectful. He, too, felt that nothing he did worked. After all, wasn't he bringing home a paycheck? What in the world did he do wrong, he thought? Ricky was demoralized both by Jean's belief that he was selfish and by his own victim thinking.

There you have it: Three reasons why blaming really boomerangs badly.

How to Stop This Awful Habit

Here are fourteen powerful things to do:
1. Believe that blaming is wrong and abusive. Hate that you have been abusive. You may be very unhappy that you didn't get what you wanted, and that is understandable; however, you have to become the type of person who wouldn't want to injure those you love. Even when you're angry.

Lenny read this chapter and he then understood. He felt great remorse about all the times he called Lenore names and he wished he hadn't blamed everything that went wrong on her. He started to recall childhood moments that he hoped to forget forever. He came to understand that blaming is absolutely wrong and he vowed never to blame again.

A month later, he and Lenore arrived at the airport to return home from visiting their children. Tickets in hand, Lenore, who made the purchase online, approached the counter. "I'm sorry, ma'am," the ticket agent said, "these are for next week." Aghast, Lenore realized that when she was on the computer, the date set to default when she went back to fix the number of passengers to "two." She was trembling when she turned to Lenny with the news. The error would cost $700 because they had to leave today, no matter what. Lenny swallowed. But he stuck to his commitment. Blame was out. "Don't worry. We're all human" was all he said.

Facing your mistakes may be painful, but having the courage to do so is a big step towards loving yourself.

(Tool 63) How to Stop Blaming #1
Believe in your heart that blaming is abusive and wrong. Reflect on how it hurt you to be blamed.

---

2. There are times when you need to bite your tongue. Literally. Just don't say anything.

Karen got so frustrated with her little toddler, Bret. But obviously, she couldn't take a time-out from her child at the mall. She realized she should stop blaming him for wanting to run around; after all, he's just a little kid. So she bit her tongue. And it worked! She exerted enough self-control to think more rationally about how to get him to cooperate.

Karen did the same thing with her husband, Jim. They were late—again— because he forgot to bring the directions. But she could have remembered to pick them up off the counter, too. She bit her tongue just as she was about to let him have it in the car. As quiet set in, she took responsibility for not remembering the directions herself. In that moment of quiet, she remembered that her phone has a GPS and she silently typed in the destination.

Stop yourself from hurting your loved one--and start to build bridges.

(Tool 64) How to Stop Blaming #2
Bite your tongue.

---

3. If you can't seem to control yourself, imagine your boss in front of you. Or someone you respect. God, maybe.

Or leave the building for a self-imposed time out. During your time out, think of something you enjoy doing, such as going fishing, shopping, whatever. Get your head somewhere else. Get in the habit of letting it go. And then congratulate yourself for being able to do that.

Karen was proud of herself for finding solutions in the quiet spaces she created while biting her tongue—but her tongue was hurting! She decided instead to concentrate on something pleasant and calming instead of starting the blame game. She had liked a little cabin in the mountains she had visited as a child. She taught herself to imagine being there, free of worries when she became stressed. Inevitably, solutions would appear in the mental space she created for herself.

Phil was about to let Sal have it when he allowed himself to imagine, actually to feel, God's presence in the room. To some extent, it was uncomfortable to think that God was actually watching him be mean to his wife. But the vision helped. And a moment later, when the blame was gone from his head, he felt as though God had applauded him for getting successfully through that moment. He felt warmed by His presence.

Taking steps to stop a bad habit can be enjoyable, even fun.

(Tool 65) How to Stop Blaming #3
Get your head into a pleasant space—think that God is watching, or reflect on a trip or hobby.

---

4. Stop blaming yourself. Victim thinking is at the root of blaming others.

Not only does victim thinking mean you believe others are dumping on you (and therefore you should attack back), but deep inside, that old tape of your parents blaming *you* is still playing. That has to stop.

The key to doing this is to learn to like yourself. Sit down and list your positive qualities. Review them again and again. When you find anything you don't like about yourself, work on a plan for self-improvement. The best protection against self-blame is self-improvement. It is possible to do! Then keep telling yourself that you *are* changing.

The only catch is that you must be sincere. You must really try to change or the whole thing won't work. If you tell yourself, "I'm only human," and you give yourself a thousand excuses for not improving, then the self-blame at the root of the other-blame will keep bothering you. Give yourself appropriate congratulations for every step forward. When you don't make the steps you want, don't be hard on yourself and don't excuse yourself either; just keep plugging.

Anthony considered himself good at picking stocks. But when he picked wrong, he would not stop beating himself up. He kept going over and over how could he make such a "stupid mistake." He was ready to toss in the towel. He took the advice in this book and decided to stop the self-blame. When the market next turned against him, he spent some time analyzing what he should have done and made plans for how he would handle the same circumstances next time. It's funny how small things make a big difference: He thought about what he would do next time instead of telling

104

himself he was a failure for not having done it this time. This changed attitude meant that instead of self-blame he was actually looking forward to the next opportunity to put his analysis to the test.

Treat mistakes as opportunities for learning rather than calls for blame.

(Tool 66) How to Stop Blaming #4
Stop blaming yourself. Work to improve yourself, but don't blame yourself when you make mistakes. Don't blame others, either. Just correct the problem and move on.

---

5. Every time your significant other seems to screw up, think of what she has done right lately and focus on that.

Focus on the good, and you will see it. Interestingly, not only will you see it more clearly, but when you notice it, your partner will feel good about it, too—and produce more of what you wanted. That is the nature of the positive; it breeds more positive. What has your partner done right?

Joshua was really irritated at the mess that Arianne seemed to generate in the house. Next time he walked in and was confronted with the mess, he immediately turned his eyes to his beloved children and smiled at how delightful they were. "Arianne has been an excellent mother, that's for sure," he told himself.

Here's a key to a long and happy marriage.

(Tool 67) How to Stop Blaming #5
Focus on the positive the other person has done. Start listing positive accomplishments.

---

6. Let's expand on the benefit of the doubt exercise introduced in Chapter One [Refer to p. 20, Tool 14]. For each screw-up, make up three reasons that are good and reasonable explanations for the screw-up, so that instead of blaming her, what you are doing is seeing her side, for a change. This is how to give the benefit of the doubt.

Arianne got into a car accident. Joshua decided to think of three reasonable explanations in order to give her the benefit of the doubt:
(1) "Wow, she really works so hard in her career, takes care of the family, gets the meals on the table, and I know my past blaming behavior has been very stressful to her. It's no wonder that she had that accident with all the stress she's under."
(2) "You know, I'll bet that accident wasn't even her fault, because when I don't rattle her, I notice that she is quite a capable person. With her friends, she's calm, cool, and collected. It's only when I start blaming her that she seems rattled."
(3) "Well, statistically, everyone is going to get into an accident some time, so I guess this was her time. It happens to the best of us."

Lillian feels Matthew neglects her because he stays so late at the office (which is victim thinking). To get out of this mindset, she tells herself, "I'll bet he had to go over those papers before turning them in to his boss, or maybe he needed some last minute data to supplement the report. It could even be that there was an error in the calculations and he had to do the whole thing over."

Now, does that mean what you're doing is excusing bad behavior on your partner's part? No! If Arianne has had the fourth accident this month and she is driving drunk, then you can't find a positive explanation. If you have evidence your husband is cheating, then finding a benign explanation for his being late again is only self-defeating.

If you only learn one tool, this is it.

(Tool 68) How to Stop Blaming #6:
Benefit of the Doubt

Come up with three to five positive explanations for what appears to be bad behavior.

---

7. Clarify exactly what you want.

People often say, "I want him to (somehow magically) know what I want." Well, he won't. People can't mind-read and shouldn't have to. Stop expecting your partner to read your mind.

Then, when the mind-reading doesn't go as you want, you might get angry. Well, that's no good. The solution is to communicate your needs in a way that makes your partner motivated to fulfill them.

Jean and Ricky

The case of Ricky and Jean is clear here. Ricky assumed that Jean should know (magically) how lonely he felt after Goldie arrived. And Jean assumed that Ricky should know (magically) how tired she was after having a baby. No, they needed to tell each other—explicitly—just how they felt, and then they needed to *ask* for what they wanted. Before the painting fiasco, the conversation could have gone like this:

Jean: Look, I am feeling awful. I am so tired. I don't know how I can hold up my end.

Ricky: But Goldie came three weeks ago. You're past labor and delivery. You're not carrying around a seven-pound weight and all that body fluid. You always used to go on very little sleep. Why are you so tired now?

Jean: I guess the baby depletes iron. I don't really know. The obstetrician told me I still have to take these pregnancy vitamins.

Ricky: Are you taking them?

Jean: Yes.

Ricky: So why aren't they working?

Jean: Well, they're not magic. I'm supposed to take them for at least one month past birth and more if I'm nursing.

Ricky: Oh, I see. But still, you used to go on just a few hours of sleep. Why is this different?

Jean: If I'm feeling energetic and I sleep well, and then I set my alarm early, I am fine. But if I'm feeling exhausted already and just as I fall into a deep sleep, Goldie wakes me up, then it's a different thing. I don't get my rest that way. Can you understand that?

Ricky: So maybe you should stop nursing.

Jean: Oh, and you're going to feed her in the middle of the night?

Ricky: I detected a note of sarcasm in your voice. That wasn't nice.

Jean: Well, here I am having to defend myself for the crime of being tired because you haven't been helping.

Ricky: You're right. I didn't understand. I didn't realize how tired you really are. I want to be a better husband. But I still don't think it's nice of you to be sarcastic just because I didn't get it.

Jean: You're right too. I'm sorry. I shouldn't have been sarcastic. So you really would do the night feeding?

Ricky: [takes a huge breath] Well, I guess so. But you know, I have to tell you, this whole thing makes me feel funny. I don't know what to do. I never had any experience with babies before.

Jean: Welcome to the club. Neither did I.

Ricky: Well, I'm a little scared. You seem to know what you're doing.

Jean: Okay. How about this? You watch me change her a few times. Then you try. Let's start with that. Any help you give would be appreciated because sometimes I'm so tired I don't know my own name.

Ricky: Okay. I can try it that way. [deep sigh again]

Jean: What's the matter now?

Ricky: To tell the truth . . . This is hard to say . . . I miss you. I miss what we had.

Jean: [far away look on her face] You're right. I didn't even think about that, but you're right. Well, let's just muddle through this, okay? They say it gets a little easier.

Ricky: I hope so.

Here, they have communicated. They communicated true feelings and actual requests. They didn't expect the other to be a mind-reader.

But they did more than that. Notice the times they agreed that the other person was right. Notice the times they didn't get defensive, but just listened to what the other person had to say. Notice Ricky's nice offer of help and Jean's acceptance. Notice the hope in this conversation, all because they've made up their minds to be kind and cooperative. Notice the great results. Being nice is really empowering.

Interestingly, it turns out that Jean was so tired that she forgot that she hadn't been spending quality time with her husband. She also realized that she missed it. So you see, by bringing it up for himself, Ricky also gave Jean something to think about. Perhaps, in a month or two, as Goldie gets older, they can find a regular babysitter and go out alone together more often. Now that she realized how she also misses having some fun, she won't be doing it to please just him, but herself as well.

Is there a solution right now? Not yet. The reality is that Goldie requires care and the time spent on her will rob Ricky and Jean of sleep and time for the togetherness they used to have. However, now they will be working as a team on their parenting and that will give them a new way of being together. They will joke when Goldie spits up on one of them and the other will rush to get the cleaning supplies. Working together like that is what will make them a team. And that will be fun. I promise.

Mindy and Sol had to learn this lesson too. Sol works hard to provide for the family. Mindy's job gets her home at a reasonable time and she makes dinner, goes over homework, tidies up the house, and oversees the bedtime routine all before Sol shows his face. Mindy has told Sol repeatedly that she doesn't like this arrangement; she doesn't like that she does everything herself. His answer has always been that he needs to work long hours to take care of the family.

On one level, Mindy agreed with him. She also realized that it wasn't so much the lack of help because he offered to take turns cooking ahead on Sundays and she liked that, but it still wasn't enough. After thinking hard about what was bothering her, she came to understand that it was the feeling of just being left alone, as if she weren't married, that really hurt. When she clarified that, Sol had an idea. The next day, right in the middle of working on a project, about 5 p.m., he called. When she answered it, he said, "I love you." Her heart started to pound. That felt really, really good. A tear came to her eye, and she knew she could get through.

Liberate yourself from wishing your partner would read your mind.

(Tool 69) How to Stop Blaming: #7
Be clear as to what you want. Be willing to give too.

---

8. Sometimes clarifying what you want isn't enough. Your partner may be really hurt and angry for the past blaming and not be willing or ready to listen and do what you want. Certainly, at the very minimum, you need to apologize. Say something like this:

> "I want you to know up front that I realize that I have been hurtful in the past, and I apologize. More importantly, not only do I apologize, but I want you to know that I deeply regret the way I sounded in the past by blaming you all the time. I really want to change, and I really want to make our relationship better."

Go back to the Ricky and Jean dialogue above. Notice how Jean says, *"You're right too. I'm sorry. I shouldn't have been sarcastic."* That's a simple apology. Here, he was the one who hurt her, yet the truth is that in this conversation, she was sarcastic and she is apologizing for it.

And, although Ricky doesn't say, "I'm sorry," he does agree that Jean is correct in the statement, *"You're right. I didn't understand. I didn't realize how tired you really are. I want to be a better husband."* In fact, this statement is close to the model above of a nice apology because he elaborates and you can tell it's heartfelt.

Cleanse yourself of those mistakes you kicked under the rug.

(Tool 70) How to Stop Blaming: #8
Apologize.

---

9. Even the apology, frankly, may not be enough. You have made your partner suffer greatly by the past blaming and you can't just make it all go away with a few sweet words. It would be like causing an auto accident in which someone died and then telling their family, "I'm sorry." Well, big deal. Words are cheap.

It may be necessary for you to go one step further: repentance. You have to do something to make up for the past, and you have to do it in a way that specifically shows two things:
➤ You realize in your bones how bad blaming is.
➤ You won't ever do it again.

This is the key method for making up for any suffering you have caused your loved ones.

One possibility is to say, "I want you to test me. How long have I gone in the past without blaming you?" Then, exceed that time limit—by a good margin.

Changing your behavior begins with a commitment. Following through is difficult, challenging, and exhilarating.

(Tool 71) How to Stop Blaming: #9
Begin the repentance process by exceeding the time limit you have ever been non-blaming to prove your sincerity that you will never blame again.

---

10. When something bothers you, it does need to be discussed—without blaming.

Ask permission. Suppose Ricky had done that with Jean when he first started to worry that she didn't want sex. Suppose he had said,

"The problem is there is something I need very much and don't

know how to get it from you. It's more important to me than you realized. Can we talk about what it is and how important it is?"

That would have gotten Jean's attention, wouldn't it?

Good manners are a respect builder.

(Tool 72) How to Stop Blaming: #10
Convey how important the issue is by asking permission to talk about it now.

---

11. Even requesting your partner's attention may not be enough to rectify the situation. She may still not understand how important it is to you. Don't forget, if your partner is going to make some changes in his behavior, it will require putting those changes high on the priority list. How do you get your partner to understand how important that change is to you?

You need to get your partner's full attention then have a separate conversation focused just on this one problem. A good way to underscore the importance to you is to ask him, "Do you understand how important this is to me?"

Kenneth wanted time to unwind when he got home, even if it was simply ten minutes alone. He liked to put away his stuff, use the bathroom, change clothes, get a glass of cold water. He wasn't asking for much, but, it never happened. He would walk in the door and be bombarded. Jen, his wife, was too preoccupied with the children to rein them in, and so full of news, questions, just the desire to talk to another adult, that she often forgot this simple request. Kenneth asked her permission to discuss "an important matter." She said "Sure." He waited until the children were in bed and there were no other distractions to make sure she really heard him. Then he said, "Can I get ten minutes when I walk in the door?"

Jen was astonished. "That's the whole thing?" she asked. "You went to all this trouble to make time to discuss this?" This is how the remainder of their dialogue went:

Kenneth: Yes.

Jen: Well, of course. No problem. Why couldn't you tell me over dinner?

Kenneth: I wanted your undivided attention because this was important to me.

Jen: Wow. It must really be important. Sorry I didn't realize it.

Here's a new idea: Make your needs important. Now, that's healing.

(Tool 73) How to Stop Blaming: #11
Set up a time to make your request with no other complications or distractions in the conversation.

---

12. Doing all these steps still might not be enough. It may be that there is an obstacle in your partner's mind that you just didn't know about. Airing all this is absolutely necessary for the success of your plan. Take the Kenneth and Jen case, above, with a little twist:

Jen, his wife, thought his request was unfair. After all, she'd been handling the kids all day. When did she get a break? Why was he more in need of that ten minutes than she was? So the conversation took a different turn:

When Ken requested the ten minutes, Jen didn't look too eager. She was silent.

Kenneth: What's the matter?

Jen: I realize you want unwinding time, but frankly, by the time you get home, I'm going nuts. I need to have adult conversation. I need to go to the bathroom for Pete's sake! I just need that ten minutes myself.

A light bulb went off in Kenneth's mind.

<u>*Kenneth*</u>*: I'll do you one better! If you just give me that ten minutes to refresh myself, I'll give you a half hour! I love playing with the kids and, frankly, I envy you the time you have with them. I'll serve supper. I'll even make it an hour and do the bath! Just give me the ten minutes. How's that for a deal?*

Obviously, Jen couldn't refuse.

Here's an empowering thought: Don't give up too quickly!

> **(Tool 74) How to Stop Blaming: #12**
> Find out what the obstacles are and negotiate.

13. When you have used all of the above tools, but there absolutely is no positive way to explain a bad behavior on your partner's part, blaming is still not the right answer. The next tool is to look for *solutions.*

Let's return to the case of Joshua and Arianne [Refer to pp. 105-106]. She had four car accidents and it turned out that she drinks. Joshua was scared out of his mind that Arianne could get killed or kill someone else behind the wheel. He used to be a patient person, but her behavior changed that. It seemed like nothing he did worked. That's why he started blaming.

What he needed to do is *get help.* Here are things that he has not tried:
➢ Special groups that deal with your partner's particular problem (e.g., Alcoholics Anonymous, Al-Anon for partners)
➢ Residential treatment centers that specialize in your partner's issue
➢ Your house of worship
➢ Friends who have gone through the same thing

➤ Couples workshops, seminars, and courses
➤ Couples therapy

That's a good beginning. Generally, each of the above resources can point you to more. Often people know specific people who have dealt with the same type of problem. You don't want to wallow in your misery. Or keep blaming.

In the case of the guy who was suspiciously late coming home every night, the thing to do would be to confront him, use surveillance methods yourself, or go ahead and hire an investigator if it is definitely not a question of you imagining things.

Your burden is immediately lightened when someone with expertise in the area shares it.

(Tool 75) How to Stop Blaming: #13
When the behavior is bad and you've tried everything, *get help.*

---

14. Finally, there is an element to all this that is totally out of human control. Sometimes, differences and problems are due to miscommunication, but often they're due to the fact that humans will make mistakes. To rehash and rehash mistakes is not only unhelpful but detrimental to health. It is best to search for new solutions, if they are there, and to otherwise deal gracefully with Life's curveballs.

Jane got into a car accident. Norman didn't say anything. He knows that "accidents happen."

Mark and Lucy were debating which college their son, Neil, should go to. They looked carefully into four of them and then made their selection. As it turned out, their son got into trouble for having pot in the dorm. They were quite surprised as they thought they had researched carefully the degree of supervision there. They decided not to blame one another for not picking up on some red flags they both missed. They put their heads together to come up with a new plan. They brought their son home and told him to get a job for the semester until he would show them he was mature enough to go to college.

Samantha worried over moving her mother into a nursing home. She went back and forth in her mind daily between the toll on her family from keeping her mother at home versus the concern for her mother's well-being in a nursing home. She finally decided on the nursing home, but on her second visit there, she discovered her mother not well cared for. She didn't blame herself; she just brought her home and started over in her search.

After two weeks of Jen allowing Kenneth space for 10 min [Refer to pp. 113-115] *when he got home, the system broke down. Jen was sick with a cold and did not have the energy or will to keep the kids off of their dad and she herself wanted some TLC. Kenneth figured that good plans do get swamped sometimes and he would wait til Jen was feeling like herself to see if the program could be restarted.*

When you've done everything, acceptance is the best stress-reducer.

(Tool 76) How to Stop Blaming: #14
Take a philosophical approach to life: Bad things sometimes "happen." Just get back to the drawing board.

Chapter Nine
Body Language Roars

"Oh, sweetie, you can talk to me any time." This is Phil, the man who controlled his temper by imagining God's presence in the room. You would think he'd come a long way in speaking to Sal, his wife. But his nose was in a book [Refer to p. 104, Tool 65].

Body language is the most ancient form of communication. People "read" it subconsciously and register it as weird when spoken language and the body aren't saying the same thing.

"I respect you," Lenny, the man who had laughed when his wife, Lenore, dropped the roast, said, looking bored, eyes cast off at a spot on the floor, one eyebrow sort of arched [Refer to pp. 65, 74 and 75 – Tools 40, 45, and 46].

What message did Lenore hear? The opposite, probably. Lenny did not realize that although he'd worked hard on his words, his body language remained insensitive.

Karen, the woman who'd learned to bite her tongue said to Bret, her toddler, "I love you" but her arms were stiff as she held him. Her mind was elsewhere [Refer to p. 103, Tool 64].

Worries about our relationships, work, finances, and health can affect a simple thing like how conscious we are when we hug our children—and they can tell.

Three years later, Joshua [Refer to pp. 105-106, 115] *was still trying not to focus on the mess that Arianne hadn't attended to. Now that she had completed rehab and was not drinking, he knew she needed positive reinforcement, but it was so hard. He was smiling at his children, the tool he used to get his mind off the mess (Tool 67). Arianne said, "I notice you're distracted. I feel so left out of your thoughts, sometimes." "Oh, no," Joshua responded quickly, picking up her hand, saying, "You mean the world to me." But he held her hand very, very loosely.*

Everyone is trying so hard to use the tools in this book – and that's good! But body language cannot be overlooked. When the body conveys an unclear meaning or one that is the opposite from the spoken one, either the words are just not believed, or the listener becomes confused.

Every day, Arianne woke up and looked in the mirror with puzzlement. "Who am I?" she wondered. At one time she thought she knew. She always used to think she was a nice person, a good person. Something turned her into a bad person, someone you wouldn't want to be around. How did that happen? She felt ugly and out of touch. She was scared, too; she could feel her heart racing. She wondered if she should be medicated. That scared her, too: She didn't want to turn into a pill junky now that she was no longer drinking.

People would rather mistrust themselves than the ones they love. Arianne doesn't need medication. She needs a husband who learns to affirm her. He's got to make peace with the mess that bothers him because his wife's sanity is more important.

Here's a key rule of words and deeds:

> ➤ If words and deeds don't match, the listener doesn't believe the words. Behavior (i.e., body language) rules. That's where the aphorism, "actions speak louder than words" comes from.

Put your body language on the same "page" as your words.

(Tool 77) Reflect on This . . .

Have you used rude or contradictory body language? Have you received it? What was it? How has it made you feel? What messages have you gotten from it?

Here's another scenario. Suppose the body language was not subtle and not contradictory. Let's say it was eyeball rolling while telling someone "That's dumb." It turns out that the eyeball rolling does more damage than the words.[1, 2, 3, 4, 5] The body language is more potent, more powerful, than even the words, hurtful as they are. So when you add them together, it packs a punch.

Body language is interpreted by a different part of the brain than words. When you receive body messages, they are read by the more emotional part of the brain (the anterior cingulate region).[6] Not only are those messages more potent and painful, they are harder to overcome years later; they are harder to counteract and harder to unlearn. (Not impossible, just harder.) This part of the brain develops in babies from birth—before they are verbal. It recognizes and reacts to body language.

That is why you somehow believe that put-downs through body-language are true. Illogically, people believe that negative messages interpreted from body language are truer than the rational and positive arguments of friends and loved ones. It's all because of where the messages are stored in the brain.

In sum, the messages conveyed by body language:
➢ Are believed more readily than speech
➢ Hurt more
➢ Are harder to get over than cognitive messages
➢ Can lead to intense self-doubt and confusion

Jean and Ricky

Let's replay the action for Jean and Ricky by just attending to body language. Ricky walks into the house. Does Jean turn around with a smile and say "hi"? No. Her back is to him and she's concentrating on her paint job. What message does that convey?

Ricky then goes into his room to lick his wounds. But that's not what his body is telling Jean. He doesn't say "Hi" either. He could have chosen to be a sport about it and said, "Nice work." No point in causing a problem now that the paint is on the wall. Or, he could have been honest and told her he was hurt. In any event, what did he tell her? He slumped off to his room. His body said, "I don't care." About you. About the paint job. About our relationship.

The next part of the story takes place in a restaurant, where Ricky is kidding around with his brother-in-law about the waitress's body. He makes a comment about the waitress's body and caps it off by laughing. Who was the joke on? What message did the laughter convey to Jean?

After this, body language is expressed by "stony silence." Jean returns from the rest room and finishes eating without a word. How in the world do you enjoy your dinner that way? Obviously, you don't. And if you're not going to enjoy it, why bother eating it? Personally, I would have called Ricky outside and told him how outraged and hurt I was. Whether she meant to or not, her body language said, "rejection, rejection, rejection."

Let's rewrite the story again. If *either one* of them had smiled and said "Hi" when Ricky came into the baby blue living room, even if they felt badly about the past, the whole thing would not have escalated. What appeared to be cold indifference expressed in their body language is what pushed a tense time over the edge.

You have the strength to be honest.

(Tool 78) Checklist

Rolling eyeballs
No eye contact
Narrowed eyes
Arched eyebrow (when sarcastic)
Look of amazement (when sarcastic)
Doing other things while listening (e.g., reading newspaper, texting)
No touch
Sarcastic tone
Cold tone
Not being there (physically present) too often
Body turned away
No smile
Inappropriate smile (e.g., at someone's pain)
Rude hand gestures
Hand gestures of anger (e.g., slapping together, banging one fist into palm of other)

Have you been guilty of non-verbal assaults? Have you experienced them?

When we think we're sending a non-verbal message of *our* hurt, what we're really doing is sending a message whose effect is to:

➢ Reject
➢ Frighten
➢ Put down

Knowing your body's messages: How do other people see you?

(Tool 79) Reflect on This . . .

What is your purpose in using abusive body language?
Are you conveying the message you want to convey? Will you be a happy person that way? Are there better ways to get across the message you really want to convey? Or are you always cajoling? Submissive? Does that work or make things worse?

Free yourself from other people's problems.

> ### (Tool 80) Reflect on This . . .
> Do you see a connection between someone's feeling down and depressed and their use of abusive body language on you? Now that you're becoming aware of it, can you see that *it isn't really about you*? That it's his problem?

Let's tie this in to anger, another form of body language. If you try to hide anger, it will show in your tone and body. Instead, you've got to get rid of it. Here's one technique: When things are going well, practice having positive feelings towards your significant other by thinking about the good things about this person. Do you remember Tool 67? You were asked to focus on the positive accomplishments of the other person. Now I'm asking you to focus on your own positive *feelings* toward the other person, regardless of overt accomplishments.

Focus intently on the positive until you feel happy inside. You might be able to use a photo of a happy occasion to help get you to that good spot. Do this exercise every day. When a bad moment comes, bring up these images and thoughts and focus on them so as to move beyond your anger.

Sometimes happiness is all about where you look.

> ### (Tool 81) Reflect on This . . .
> What images and ideas about your partner bring a smile to your face? Can you practice focusing on them?

Perhaps the most prevalent kind of abusive body language is yelling. Simply by raising your voice, you can raise another person's blood pressure. It's powerful—and damaging. Read on.

Chapter Ten
Scaring into Submission

Dina kept turning her tissue around and around in her hand. She was trying to describe how fights with her husband, David, escalate. "It's when he gets a certain look in his eye that I become really frightened," she said.

The unconscious mind picks up threatening body language even when we are not consciously aware of it. Surely, then, how very uncomfortable we feel when someone overtly uses scary body language.

What are the different ways someone can make a face that is frightening?
- Angry eyes
- Grim mouth
- Baring teeth
- Taut muscles or tendons at the neck or forehead
- Flaring nostrils
- Red flush

And that's just the face. How about the voice? There are harsh tones; there's yelling; and one little girl, thinking of her parents, (correctly) pointed out that there is a difference between yelling and screaming. It's awfully sad that she could make such a distinction.

And then there is the rest of the body: tense muscles, rapid heartbeat, sweat.

"Even when my husband is joking, I know that he is angry if his neck gets red," Dina added.

Start to think about things that used to be subconscious.

> **(Tool 82) Reflect on This . . .**
> Which of the menacing body language messages above do you think is worse? Why?

One reason some men may be particularly scary is because they seem to be lusting for a fight. Researchers put monitors on men who were in a lab having conversations with their wives. These couples had volunteered for the research because the men were verbally abusive. What the researchers found was that most of the men would indeed show all the body signs of being upset when arguing with their wives—high blood pressure, rapid pulse, shallow breathing—but there was a percentage that would *improve* during conflicts. In other words, where an argument would be a source of stress for most people, for this small group of men, the argument was actually a way they *relieved* stress. Such men would probably look for conflict just to relieve the tension they felt. The researchers' conclusion: Beware of these men.[1] Because conflict made their vital signs get better, men of this type might be dangerous. Thus, spouses should tune in to their abusers' body language and be aware of the *type* of man they have because the type that feels better during conflict may not be someone who will want to learn to reduce that conflict.

I wouldn't automatically give up on such a person. In spite of his relief from stress when he fights, he may still want to overcome this. Once he understands how he functions, he may want to work on himself. Nevertheless, it is important to be aware of potential danger.

There are scary women, too. Murray Straus, the University of New Hampshire researcher, found that women can be cruel verbally just as often as men. The difference between the sexes? When men are intent on injuring, their physical superiority means they will cause more damage.[2]

Seeing yourself as others see you is an eye-opener.

> **(Tool 83) Reflect on This . . .**
> Does your partner scare you? What does he do? Are you scary? What do you do? Do you want to be that kind of person? Should that be the basis for your relationship?

Physical effects of hearing yelling

Hearing yelling, especially being yelled at yourself, causes *fear*. Fear affects the brain[3] differently from other emotions. It creates a temporary state of physical arousal. If the source of fear continues, it can make you ill.

That is why domestic violence is women's top health issue at an annual medical cost of more than fifty million dollars.[4] Abused women have more internal medicine, gastroenterological, gynecological, and other health complaints than people who are not mistreated. In fact, women report these medical complaints more frequently than they report the bruises they receive from being beaten.[5] The bruises heal, but the stress-related problems last.

Other known effects of the stress in an abusive home are elevated measures of anxiety, depression, obsessive-compulsive disorder, post-traumatic stress disorder, bipolar disorder, and suicidal ideation.[6, 7]

We would expect such effects from physical violence. However, research comparing the effects of physical violence and emotional abuse indicate that emotional abuse results in a *greater* level of traumatic symptoms.[8, 9] In fact, researchers in biological psychiatry have shown that childhood maltreatment prematurely shortens our DNA![10]

The fear generated "just" from being yelled at triggers the fight or flight response[11, 12] That is why it is child abuse for children to hear their parents yelling at each other.[13]

Apparently, being yelled at alone is more stressful and more damaging to the body and the brain—at any age—than even domestic violence.

Dina was having trouble sleeping. She was waking up at the sound of a leaf falling. Every time she heard a little noise, even during the day, she jumped. David never put her down. He kept telling her he loved her, and indeed, he showered her with gifts, trips, and attention. But she had learned early in their marriage not to cross him. Even that wasn't good enough. She walked on eggshells, but any little slip and the yelling would start. He was working on himself now. He had stopped yelling at her two months ago. Dina had circled the last episode on her calendar. But he had an office in the house and she could hear him yelling on the phone. It wouldn't stop. And it unnerved her.

Listen to your body: It's telling you something.

(Tool 84) Reflect on This . . .
Have you ever been diagnosed with an anxiety disorder? Are you taking medication for stress? Blood pressure problems? Consider this: Maybe you wouldn't need medication if the yelling would stop. What is your body telling you about your relationship?

Why Do People Yell?

Yelling is one of the most self-defeating behaviors. Check out this scene: He yells. Now she's mad, so *she* yells. Well, he is *really* mad, so now he *really* yells. Where is this going? Nowhere.

It can't, because they're not getting to the heart of their issue [14] as Murray Straus explained in his extensive research on conflict. In fact, the more they yell, the more they move *away* from the issue. They add intimidation to anger, mistrust, walls, and bad feelings. Where does it end? Often in divorce court or death. Neither one is necessary.

Yelling is a primitive means of getting attention. Babies cry. They're born to cry. When a baby cries, a caring parent feeds, diapers, burps, washes, holds, or sings to that baby. The cry was a good thing because babies were created to have a relationship with a caregiver such that the caring goes in one direction, from adult to child. The adult, if emotionally healthy, nevertheless feels fulfilled from giving.

As children get older, parents are expected to socialize and civilize them. Parents explain to their children that yelling and screaming are not necessary; now that they have learned to speak, they can ask for what they want, but many adults never outgrow their childhood tantrums.

Taking an honest look at yourself is tough, but doesn't it feel good to have done it?

(Tool 85) Reflect on This . . .
Any yelling is too much. How often do you or your partner yell? Do you feel like you're sending the message you want?

How Yelling Backfires

Yelling makes things worse in three ways:
➢ First, since yelling is an emotional response, it usually requires that the listener guess at the real meaning behind it.
➢ Second, yelling intimidates the listener so that even if the words are clear, and even if the listener does exactly what is requested, the listener does not act from the heart. How could he? So in getting what she wants, the yeller paradoxically is *preventing* what she wants, which is love, trust, respect, and validation.
➢ Third, yelling invokes anger in retaliation, so the targeted person, now good and angry, retaliates.

Another side effect is that people who yell are estranged from themselves. Since the yelling has replaced reason and communication, they haven't thought through what is bothering them, why, and what to do about it. This frustrates them more because they still want something, although they really aren't too clear on what it was. So, by force of habit, they take it out on their partners who, after all, *should* know what they want—just like their parents should have known what they wanted when they were little. But their significant other is not a mind reader and doesn't necessarily know. And at this point, it's moot anyway, since that significant other feels rejected and angry and no longer cares.

If you acknowledge the first question, work hard on the second one: It will yield a wealth of information.

```
(Tool 86) Reflect on This . . .
Have you pushed away the people you love by yelling?

Do you know why you yell?
```

Stopping Once and for All Time

If we agree that yelling will put a separation between you and those you love and *prevent* you from getting your needs met, then it's time to stop.

Here are ten steps to take control of your yelling.

Get a handle on what your stressors are.

```
(Tool 87) How to Stop Yelling #1
Can you tell right away when you are under stress or does it
have to build up first? How do you usually react to stress?
Can you think under stress, or do you just react emotionally?
What helps you to be able to think? Start taking note of what
stresses you and what de-stresses you.
```

Step two will fool you. You will think it is too simple to be as powerful as it actually is. It is the best-known and least understood de-stressor: breathing. The intelligent, thinking part of your brain is located in a completely separate place (the cerebral cortex) from the emotional part (the limbic system). But the emotional part is programmed to respond first. Deep breathing reduces emotional reactivity by slowing down your autonomic nervous system, the trigger-quick responses you don't want. So, every day, at times when things are going smoothly, practice taking deep, slow breaths.

Tom is a big husky guy. He drives a truck for a very good company. When he's on the road, he feels like a king—and nobody bothers him. But when he's home, it's a different story. Yet, he loves Linda, his wife of twenty years. He's tired of the fighting and the yelling which doesn't accomplish anything. He and Linda consulted with me, but when I suggested deep breathing, he thought that was a little kooky, not in his comfort zone. On the other hand, Linda made the logical point that you could practice any time including on the road as long as he didn't listen to the CD while driving. No one would have to know. He decided to go ahead and practice while traveling, when he's already calm, just to enjoy that process. Back at home, it became automatic for him to draw some nice, deep breaths when a loaded topic came up.

Deep breathing is more potent than you think.

> **(Review Tool 6) How to Stop Yelling #2**
> Practice deep breathing every day.

Step three takes the breathing further. It involves your entire body. It is called progressive relaxation. If your body is relaxed, you will not be stressed. The two are incompatible. Therefore, this technique, when combined with the deep breathing, will be more powerful than medication for stress and without the side effects. It puts you in charge of your mind and your body.

Please note that there is one caveat: You must practice both of these exercises daily for at least a few weeks before you will start to notice that they can work to avert a fight when you get tense. For some people, it could take several months of practice before they can get their emotions under control. But isn't it worth it?

Download your additional tools at www.TheHealingIsMutual.com/ download. The relaxation audio has gotten rave reviews.

LaShonda has a long car ride to work with a lot of traffic. She decided to focus on relaxing her entire body from head to toe right there in the car, getting all the kinks out. (However, she must not listen to a relaxation CD while driving.) She finds that her trip not only stopped being frustrating, but she looks forward to it. As a bonus, her mind gets to wander a bit and she discovers, much to her surprise, that during what looked like lost time, she thinks of great ideas for work, finds solutions for family issues, and generally is quite mentally productive.

Take a sweet ten minutes for yourself

> **(Tool 88) How to Stop Yelling #3**
> Practice progressive relaxation every day: In a comfortable position, allow each part of your body to relax, starting with your scalp and working down to your toes. Take ten minutes to give yourself the relaxation of your life!

Step four takes the last two steps, and, like different instruments adding richness to a musical piece, adds a third, powerful component: visualization.

Patrick lives in the inner city. He rejected the drugs, the crime, and the street values. But he wants something better for himself and his family and he wants it badly. He knows his tension isn't getting him there. He decides to spend ten minutes every morning, getting up just a little earlier, doing the deep breathing, the relaxation, and the following visualization: He sees himself in an office building, working in a corporate law firm, wearing a nice suit. He sees himself preparing for a client. He can hear himself saying impressive things. He can smell the fresh leather upholstery in his office as he sits there. His hand wanders over his imagined desk and touches his nameplate. He feels proud, good, relaxed, and ready for work.

Whatever anger he might have had is gone.

You deserve something good.

(Tool 89) How to Stop Yelling #4
Visualize happy, self-nurturing activities while relaxing.

Would you like to fish? Swim? Hike in the mountains? Ski? Where ever, or whatever, practice enjoying "being" in that scene and go to it while you do the deep breathing.

Step five is a departure from these first steps. The first four steps are all actions, things to do. Step five combines action with a way of *looking at life.* I want you to consider shifting your focus from the negative to the positive. "Easier said than done," you'll say. Well, you're right! It isn't easy—but it is possible.

Stephen said to me, "When I walk into a room, I see what's wrong with it! See your desk, DrDeb? It's driving me crazy because it's bowed and I wonder if it will break!" Stephen will have to work hard to overcome this. However, in the course of our conversation, he admitted that when he sees his children playing, so full of fun, so carefree, his heart fills with joy. He loves attending his son's baseball games, and I told him to take some good pictures at the next game and post those around the house and in his car. He then should look at the photos whenever he feels stressed so as to bring him back to good moments in his life.

Were there wonderful and happy moments in your life that can alter your mood? Notice in our example above, the memories don't have to be related to the source of the stress.

Create an album of good memories in your mind.

(Tool 90) How to Stop Yelling #5
Put yellow sticky notes in several strategic places—the bathroom mirror, on and inside the refrigerator, on the TV, on your dashboard—using words that will help you remember the positive moments in your life.

Step six will be fun: Play with your voice; practice speaking softly or even whispering and see the reaction.

Mrs. Stenofsky came in with her two children. "My husband isn't able to be here," she said, "but basically, the problem is we all yell. That's all we do. When we want to make a point, the volume goes up and then up some more." I had a simple solution: Whisper. "What?" she exclaimed, probably thinking I was crazy. But I could see the children giggling at the thought. She started laughing, too, realizing how great it would be if they could turn this around.

A week later, they came in, and Mrs. Stenofsy reported, wide-eyed, that they were all actually able to talk to each other this week. Lydia, the elder child, chimed in, "Yeah, the first time, we couldn't hear her, so we all got quiet to listen! And that's how we really could tell how nice it was to not yell."

"Dad even did it," Mordy, the younger child, commented. "It was so weird." They all laughed.

Realize the power of a whisper.

(Tool 91) How to Stop Yelling #6
Practice speaking softly or even whispering when you want to make a point and notice the reaction.

Step seven gets back to the point made earlier that people think, for some inexplicable reason, that their partners can read their minds. When that doesn't happen, they get angry. And they have trouble figuring out for themselves what, exactly, they want and why they yell about it. There is only one way to get around this: spend some time soul-searching.

Before he started doing the breathing exercise, Tom, the truck driver, would come home from a long stretch on the road, walk in the door and almost immediately, start yelling. One time it was, "Why isn't dinner ready? You know I'm starved when I get home." Linda, his wife, knew that, obviously. But how could she know when exactly he would be home? Some days, she wasn't even sure what day he'd be home, let alone what time. And even if he called her ahead, how could that give her the time to get dinner made? And even if she could have made the dinner, the real question is, why was he yelling?

Tom had to stop and think about this. Why, exactly did that call for yelling? He took some deep breaths and thought about it. Yes, what, exactly about this made him so angry? He realized that it brought up old feelings of shifting for himself practically his whole life. He wanted to feel special. He thought dinner being ready would make him feel special. With it not being ready, he felt lonely even though he had come home.

We can suspect that if Tom was responsible for himself most of his life, his early childhood may have been neglectful. He may never have gotten the nurturing and care that children need. Although he may not be thinking of wanting to be treated like a child, this may be the ingredient he's missing. The problem is that spouses can never fill the role of parents for their partners, nor should they. For one thing, they can't mind-read or guess what their partner wants the way a parent has to figure out what's bothering a small child. Furthermore, no matter how much spouses try to do, that empty spot in the soul doesn't make up for a lost childhood. In spite of this, it is amazing how much healing *can* take place once the adult recognizes his missed childhood needs and conveys that to his partner. Some little things a partner could do may be symbolically very nurturing as you will see with Tom and Linda.

Nothing compares to the love, warmth, and friendship of an equal partnership in a marriage.

(Tool 92) How to Stop Yelling #7
Reflect on This . . .

Moving away from being upset because your partner is not a mind reader makes you more of an equal to each other. The mind reader way is more like a parent-child relationship. Which would you rather have?

Step eight requires being able to let your partner know what you don't like. When this is spelled out in a calm and friendly manner instead of by yelling, the partner is usually happy to comply. Whatever you do, never, ever, have more than three complaints on your list. Sometimes it is hard to pin down just what the problem is. Keep a journal so after a while you will see a pattern. Be aware, however, that if you start dwelling on the negatives, your life will look hopeless. This exercise is only for the purposes of communicating what bothers you. This exercise is one among many: Keep it in proportion!

Monica alternated between crying and screaming at Max. The problem was that when he asked her what he could do to aggravate her less, she didn't know. She decided to create a journal. She called it the "what annoys me" journal and realized that Max did one thing that drove her crazy: He spoke for her. No matter who they were talking to, he always assumed that she felt just as he did on the subject and said, "We feel [x]." She felt like he took away her whole Self when he did that.

Foster respect by letting your partner know—tactfully—what's bothering you.

(Tool 93) How to Stop Yelling #8

Know what you like and don't like that your partner does. Keep the list of positives a lot longer than the list of negatives and make sure the latter list has no more than three items on it—and only deal with one at a time.

When you can see patterns amidst chaos, you can sort it out.

(Tool 94) How to Stop Yelling #9

Keep a journal to help clarify your thoughts and to see patterns.

If you have worked on all the preceding steps, step ten should not be difficult. I am asking you to have a real conversation with your partner. You will want to do the deep breathing, the relaxation, and perhaps even the visualization before and during this conversation.

Tom felt kind of strange explaining to Linda what it meant to him to have dinner on the table. "See," he said, "to me, dinner is family. No dinner is alone." His simple statement was eloquent. Now Linda understood, but she wondered how she could have dinner ready with short notice. They decided that the two of them could prepare meals on weekends and freeze them. Then all Linda would have to do would be to heat it up, add a salad, and it would be complete.

When Monica told Max that what bothered her the most was how he always answered for her, it was hard for him to change. Having grown up an orphan, he had an idealized image of married life. He thought a happy couple agreed on everything; therefore, he believed that whatever he felt would be fine with her. Nevertheless, he worked on this and Monica's screaming decreased dramatically. Moreover, because she became clear on what it was that bothered her, she was able to remind Max more calmly when he slipped. The funniest thing: After Max got into the habit of saying, "What do you think, Monica?" nine times out of ten, she really did see things the same way.

Ricky and Jean
Let's get back to our main characters, Ricky and Jean. Not only did they yell, but they could not calm down enough to follow any of the other suggestions in the preceding chapters *until* they had mastered the steps on not yelling. For Ricky, being negative was his primary obstacle, but he really liked the breathing, the relaxation, and the visualization. Let's write a new chapter to their story:

Ricky readily agreed that spelling out the problem and being equals is far more enjoyable than yelling or sulking, so he and Jean had a heart-to-heart talk, and they decided to buy new paint—in mint green, a color they both loved. They realized that the blue would always be a reminder of a bad time for them, and a new paint job was something they could do together. With the counselor's help, they also planned to set aside time every week to be together in a relaxed way once that project was finished. They also planned to start saving their money toward a hot tub. They realized that although Jean might sometimes be too tired for sex, the hot tub would certainly be relaxing for both of them, and who knows? It could put them in the right mood.

Jettison the negativity and discover the friend in your partner.

(Tool 95) How to Stop Yelling #10
When you are not angry, have a civil conversation about what upsets you. Handle it in a positive manner.

Chapter Eleven
Rejecting, Neglecting, and Cheating

Joshua [Refer to pp. 119-120] *had fallen into an awful trap. In avoiding the mess in the house, he was completely avoiding Arianne, his wife. When he held her hand, it was without passion. He avoided the stains on the kitchen table by reading the paper at the table. He was already glued to his computer most of the day because of business. They lived under one roof, but Joshua had emotionally dumped Arianne.*

Neglect is dangerous because without reconnecting with your partner, you are liable to lose your feelings for her. Making that connection—and making it often—is essential to a loving marriage.

It is not a big step from simple neglect to infidelity. People don't have affairs in order to injure their partner. Maybe it feels that way, but inflicting wounds on their partner is the last thing on their minds. Usually, they're thinking of their own bad feelings: They feel they don't get enough attention or enough fun.

Neglect and cheating are not only related, they are also devastating.

Joshua stopped thinking about Arianne. She was not on his horizon. When she spoke to him, he mumbled meaningless responses. Joshua felt alone. He didn't realize it was his own doing. That's when Chu Hua walked into his office. She was exquisitely beautiful, impeccably dressed, and knew what she wanted. And she was single. Joshua kept his behavior very professional, but, mentally, he became obsessed with Chu Hua. He also felt terribly guilty. Not only was he aware that thoughts like this easily lead to affairs, but Joshua's religious values convinced him that even his thoughts were wrong.

Why would someone reject and neglect a partner?
➢ Fear of intimacy

People have become brainwashed to believe that intimacy is the equivalent of sex. Hogwash! However, let's assume that this is accurate and take this idea to its logical conclusion. If intimacy equals sex, then a person looking at porn on the computer and having a strong sexual reaction must have just experienced intimacy, right?

Wrong.

So let's begin with a better definition of intimacy. The Latin root of the word is "intimus," meaning, "innermost." On a physical level, this word does fit with the sex act itself. But when people think of their "innermost being," they are thinking of something more than just their bodies. They are thinking of their souls.

People seeking true intimacy want to be known. We want to be understood and appreciated for who we are. Sex without it becomes mechanical and meaningless.

The reality is that we don't know ourselves very well, let alone our partners. And we certainly don't know the model who had to have suffered her own trauma to "perform" on the screen. Not a little and certainly not intimately.

So why have so many people bought into this idea? I think it's simple. Ricky, for one, would have been a good candidate for observing porn. He learned from his mother that women are not to be trusted. How then would a man like him have the courage to enter into a relationship with a woman with whom he could be vulnerable?

Casual sex, on the other hand, would serve Ricky as a good substitute for real intimacy. In fact, that's what he was looking for from his wife.

If the real meaning of intimacy is to know another person's innermost self, then to be known, you have to share all kinds of things about yourself, including what frightens you, what hurts you, what you did that you think is stupid, and the parts of your character about which you're not proud. That means you have to be vulnerable. Is Ricky ready to do that? Well, he certainly hasn't as of yet in our story.

Any form of distancing from intimacy—whether it's working late hours or having casual affairs—will feel protective to someone who is unsure of whether she can trust the opposite sex, or anybody, for that matter.

What roadblocks to intimacy do you put up?

(Tool 96) Reflect on This . . .

Do you trust the opposite sex? Are you afraid to be vulnerable? Do you see yourself distancing from your partner as a result? What do you do to create that distance from intimacy? What can you do to overcome it?

➢ Loss of commonality

People may say that they no longer have anything in common. They're not afraid of intimacy; on the contrary, they would love to have a relationship with someone to whom they could open up. That person just doesn't happen to be the one they're married to. So they decide there is no gain in paying attention, talking, exchanging ideas, or being romantic. It's pointless.

That's what happened to Joshua. He let his "knowing" of his wife slip in back of the computer somewhere where the wires are tangled on the floor. And he didn't bother to reach for it. But that is precisely what is necessary: reaching for it; making an effort.

Take a look at the chart below. How many questions about your partner you can answer?

The other half of knowing yourself is knowing your other half.

(Tool 97) Checklist: Do you know your partner?

Q	A
1. What is your partner's favorite season? Why?	
2. What is your partner's favorite color for clothing?	
3. What is your partner's favorite color on the walls?	
4. What is your partner's favorite actor or actress? (or book or TV show?)	
5. What is your partner's biggest fear?	
6. What does your partner enjoy for breakfast?	
7. What is your partner's biggest worry at work?	
8. What is it your partner likes (or dislikes, or both) about his work?	
9. What is the relationship of your partner to her parents? How did it get that way?	
10. How does your partner feel about/toward his closest-in-age sibling? Why?	
11. What is your partner's best skill in the house?	
12. What is your partner's favorite leisure time activity?	
13. What skill does your partner want to learn?	
14. What activity has your partner wanted to do but is too scared to?	
15. What is your partner's biggest goal in life?	
16. Where would your partner really want to live?	
17. Why is your partner so close to her best friend?	
18. What is your partner's feeling about your mother? Why? What does she want you to do about it?	
19. In what ways do you and your partner agree on handling the children?	
20. In what ways do you and your partner disagree on handling the	

children?	
21. What are your partner's top three desires for your children?	
22. What words does your partner never want to hear from you?	
23. What words does your partner love to hear from you?	
24. When the going gets tough, does your partner want you to come up with solutions, or just listen, or something else? What?	
25. In order to improve the intimacy in your relationship, what has your partner asked you to do or say or not to do or say?	
26. What are the top three things your partner would like you to do differently to make the relationship better?	
27. Does your partner get seasick?	
28. Does your partner like to travel?	
29. Does your partner take cream in his coffee?	
30. Does your partner prefer the thermostat warmer or cooler?	
31. Does your partner prefer red wine or white wine? Or no wine?	
32. Is your partner a night or morning person?	
33. Are you and your partner on the same page spiritually? What's different? What's the same?	
34. Is your partner satisfied with your contribution to the home and family? Why yes or why not?	
35. List the values you and your partner definitely agree on.	
36. What values do you disagree on? Can you find a middle ground?	
37. Is your partner ethical when it comes to money?	
38. What is your partner's biggest secret?	
39. What is your partner's most vulnerable point?	
40. What was your partner's childhood like?	

41. What is your partner's morning routine? That is, what does he do upon awakening and at what time? Then what is next? And next after that?	
42. What is your partner's evening routine?	
43. What sorts of chores, activities, etc. would your partner never do? (e.g., talk on the phone while driving, etc.)	
44. What are her preferences regarding time spent with friends?	
45. What would your partner never do in public?	
46. What would your partner never want you to do in public?	
47. What did your partner like about his latest purchase?	
48. What did your partner not like about her latest purchase?	
49. What kinds of items does your partner like to buy?	
50. What is the reason your partner gives for being on the phone so much or so little?	

Next, what you need to do is compare answers. If you *think* you know your partner, maybe you don't. Discuss your checklists. Here's the best part of this exercise: I want you to monitor how you *feel* as you have the discussion about each of your answers. Do the revelations of things you thought you knew, but didn't, surprise you? Does your partner now seem like a more interesting person? If you now feel even a spark of interest, then that is what you must build on. This will clearly mean that it's not true that you have nothing in common, but that you have lost touch. The object is to regain that connection.

➤ Self-centeredness

If, after having an extensive conversation based on filling out this checklist, you have no interest in the answers your partner gives you at all, then the problem could simply be that you are self-centered. That is, in order for intimacy to flourish, one must *want* to get to know another person. When that interest is lacking, it could mean that your main interest is yourself. You find members of the opposite sex interesting when those people are interested in *you*. When a person is self-centered, all benefits are filtered through the screen of, "What is good for me?" as opposed to, "What is interesting about this other person?"

Self-centeredness may be the hardest of all the personality quirks to overcome. Desire to overcome it can't originate in the neglected partner; rather, the self-centered person must want to overcome it and then be willing to work hard at doing so. Since its origin is being spoiled as a child, the now-spoiled adult needs to be willing to give up being the center of the universe so as to become a fully-functioning person. That's a hard call, but all things are possible if a person wants to make them happen.

To overcome selfishness, one must make a practice of giving to others. That giving must be accompanied by a good feeling as though you were receiving those benefits yourself. To do this, use your imagination. When you give someone something—whether it is a physical thing, or an effort you've made, or even a compliment—imagine receiving that benefit. Then, holding on to the good feeling associated with it, put yourself in the place of the recipient: Imagine *being* the recipient. That's how you teach yourself to feel good as a giver. If the item or benefit or compliment is something you think the other person would want but it is not one *you* would want, just mentally substitute something you would want. Practice doing this five or more times daily and you can get rid of selfishness.

This one's tough but you can do it!

(Tool 98) Reflect on This . . .

Is selfishness your problem? Or your partner's? How do you know? Do you want to change? What steps will you take? Can you become a giver? Imagine giving generously to your partner and put yourself in his place to enjoy the process.

> Being Unmotivated

Unlike selfishness, the unmotivated person would like to give to a partner. The unmotivated person may feel badly herself. But the problem is inertia. It just doesn't seem possible to lift the relationship out of the mud. There are two ways to cure this. First, I would like you to believe, as I do, that many of the people who seem lazy may not be. They may just lack the tools to make things better. That is why I wrote this book—to put tools into your hands—and theirs. When a person doesn't know where to begin, sometimes it's easier to sit down and watch television. When you think of someone as lazy, your attitude is judgmental and condemning. When you think of him as unmotivated due to a lack of tools, it doesn't seem insurmountable.

The other cure is for true laziness and it must come from within. I can't give it to you. You would need to resolve to roll up your sleeves and do what it takes. Have you been using all the tools in this book? Are you working on understanding your partner? Do you understand yourself? The benefits far outweigh the work it will take to get there. The cost of saving a marriage—and having a good marriage as a result—is much less than the cost of a divorce, both economically and emotionally. Use that as a motivator!

Finding what motivates you is like being on a treasure hunt.

```
(Tool 99) Reflect on This . . .
What will be your motivator to get you to work on your
marriage? List possibilities.
```

> Feeling hurt

Victim thinking is at the bottom of the bad feelings that people often use to justify ignoring their partner or cheating on her.

People don't suddenly start hurting their partner out of the clear blue sky. First they feel that they've been mistreated themselves. That creates the excuse they need to go lick their wounds by indulging in something they want.

One woman complained that her husband sat on the couch all day watching TV or sleeping. He didn't work. Naturally, she was upset with this behavior. But should she have cheated? "Well, he didn't meet my needs," she said. "I'm not surprised," I replied, "since your description sounds like he was depressed. Depressed people don't have it in them to reach out to others; they can't even reach out to themselves."

This woman suffered from victim thinking. She saw her husband's behavior as a lack of interest in her when, in reality, he was the one that was suffering and needed a helping hand.

Her behavior does sound like selfishness, doesn't it? But when you talk to people who were unfaithful they might say things like, "My partner stopped making my dinner." "My partner would complain, complain, complain." "My partner was out late himself." They would always begin by finger-pointing. In fact, finger-pointing is a great clue that underneath everything is victim thinking.

Taking action is a great cure for playing victim.

> **(Tool 100) Reflect on This . . .**
> Have you given up on the marriage because your feelings are hurt? Instead of sulking, can you take the proactive steps I'm describing? List them.

Chapter Twelve
Build Barriers to Backsliding

"This time will be different," David pleaded [Refer to p. 125]. *"I really will try. I promise." David was talking about his constant yelling. He was one of the most uptight men Dina, his wife of twenty years, had ever known. But all she said was, "Yeah, I've heard that one before. What will be different this time?" She was so sad because she vaguely recalled that at one time, way, way back, she had loved him, or she thought she did.*

Dina was right. If David doesn't put in place barriers, he could easily backslide. It's human nature. It takes five steps to insure against backsliding—and David needs to use them.

1. Understand—deeply— why what you've done hurts.
2. Admit you have done wrong.
3. Hate what you've done but love yourself.
4. Resolve never to do it again, no matter what.
5. Fight against victim thinking.

1. Understand—Deeply—Why What You've Done Hurts

There are two ways to understand something. One is because someone told you. For example, the child is told, "Don't go into the street." The child doesn't know physics, doesn't know about the impact of a car hitting you at twenty mph or more. The child *does* know his dad said not to go there and the sound of his father's voice made it clear he was serious. So on some level, the child knows not to go in the street.

Then there's the knowing that goes with the "Aha!" The light bulb goes on. Something happens; the person really gets it, like suddenly understanding a physics equation or unexpectedly comprehending a partner's pain. This is the level of knowing that you must acquire in order to not damage someone again.

So, if you've read Part II, read it again! And if you have read it twice, read it three times! Use the tools. The goal is to *feel* it the way the person you hurt feels it. That is true compassion.

Feeling compassion draws you closer in a painful yet wonderful way.

(Tool 101) Reflect on This . . .
List ten things that injure your partner; explain why.

---

2. Admit You Have Done Wrong

Admitting you have done wrong is the hardest thing to do, especially for adults who were wounded in childhood. The injured party is always used to being, well, the injured party. It is shocking, disconcerting, and disturbing to learn that you have been hurting someone you love when all that time you thought you were the one who was hurt. Doesn't matter. If you hurt someone, you've got to own up to it.

As a child, Liora's mom didn't make her lunches or brush her hair. Even worse, she beat her. Liora vowed never to treat anyone like that. *And she hasn't. But sometimes her temper is short. Sometimes, she's just not pleasant. Sometimes she screams. She didn't become the same* kind *of abuser as her own parents were but she became an abuser.*

You could be saying, "Deb, I do *not* do that!" I don't call my wife names. I never scream. What's more, my parents weren't that bad either." So I'll ask you to tell me what happened that was distressing, growing up. You may come back quickly, "My dad cheated. And we all knew." Aha. So you don't think that's emotional neglect? How often was your dad home? Another question: When he *was* home, how much of his mental energy was focused on *you*—your homework, your sports, your music, your achievements, your friends? And your mom, the injured party, how much of *her* mental energy was left for you? See where I'm going? Now, with this bad role model, how much of *your* mental energy do you spend on your family? Notice the connection? So are you one of those moms or dads who's not there? Do you hide behind the computer screen? Do you maybe have a fling online?

Ricky and Jean

Ricky will have a hard time with this one. From his point of view, *he's* the one that's neglected and rejected. Sure, he injured his wife—and he is genuinely sorry for that. "But" he'll say, "she pushed my buttons." On the one hand, it's a lame excuse. On the other, that is the way he sees the world. That's because he never got past seeing himself as the target of bad treatment. If he sees himself this way, it's easy to see himself as mistreated in all his relationships, his marriage being no exception.

How do we get Ricky to see that Jean didn't push his buttons? That his marital maltreatment was in his head from the get-go? In Chapter One and Two of this book, Ricky and Jean gave their history to a counselor. The counselor did not see her job as merely providing an evaluation of the marriage. Her job was to help Ricky get past both his "poor me" and his cruelty. That is both healing medicine and preventive medicine.

Let us suppose the therapist decided to see Jean and Ricky alone once or twice and the rewrites that I made up earlier did not happen [Refer to pp. 78, 88, 107-109, 138]. The therapist is skilled and knows that the best therapy with an abuser is gentle therapy. If she is too confrontative, she will lose him; it will feel like he is being attacked or blamed and he will shut down. Nevertheless, she also knows that patient and kindly questioning can get him to look at himself more. Her most difficult challenge will be to get Ricky to realize that he has perpetuated the role of victim in his own mind and then used it as an excuse to hurt his wife.

This is how their session goes:

Therapist: Hi, Ricky. I'm glad you came back.

Ricky: Well, I didn't have much choice, you know. My wife's unhappy; so am I. She's ready to get a divorce.

Pause. What does this tell you? It tells us that Ricky is still thinking like a victim and that this thinking permeates all his relationships. Instead of thinking of the counseling as an opportunity to make his marriage—and his life—better, he is thinking that he has two rotten choices, divorce or counseling, so this is the lesser of two evils. That sentence is victim thinking. This actually presents a golden opportunity for the therapist.

Therapist: Ah. So counseling isn't something you'd ordinarily want?

Ricky: [laughing] No offense meant, ma'am, but no.

Therapist: Hmm. Well, I'm not sure what to say. I was hoping . . . [pause long enough for Ricky to contribute, but he doesn't.] I was hoping you would think of this as a way to figure out how to avoid this sort of problem again. [pause]

Ricky: [silence]

Therapist: Do you think we could do that?

Ricky: I guess so. What did you have in mind?

Therapist: Well, the way it works, the way I have been pretty successful with it with other people, is to begin with not just looking at what you did, but what you thought. It's amazing, but sometimes our thoughts control us more than we realize.

[Ricky is looking very attentive, so that's a good sign.]

So, if we can go back, way to the beginning after Goldie was born. Can you remember when you first asked Jean for sex and she declined? Can you remember that conversation?

Ricky: Yeah, actually, I can. [He proceeds to describe what he said and what Jean replied.]

Therapist: Okay. Now, can you remember what you were thinking?

[Ricky has a far-away look on his face as he recalls the difficulty of that conversation.]

Ricky: I was thinking, "S—t, she doesn't want me."

Therapist: Can you see Jean's face in your memory?

Ricky: Yes, I can.

Therapist: What expression was on it?

Ricky: Distant.

Therapist: Was it an expression of disgust, like you made her want to throw up?

Ricky: No.

Therapist: Was it an expression of anger, like she would take off your head for asking?

Ricky: Oh, no. No way.

Therapist: Was it an expression of hate?

Ricky: No, I don't really think so.

Therapist: So this expression is "distant." Not disgust, not anger, not hate.

Ricky: Yes, I would say that. [His voice is a little hesitant. His original *premise of being rejected is starting to slowly crumble.]*

Therapist: Mmm. So, you're with Jean all together how many years?

Ricky: Six.

Therapist: So, in the six years you've known her, what is usually the reason she would have that type of expression, "distant," on her face?

Ricky: [strong again] That's when she's giving me the cold shoulder.

Therapist: So every time you see that expression, you believe it's because she's giving you the cold shoulder.

Ricky: Yes. It is. I know it.

Therapist: Have you ever discussed it? Did you ever ask if that's what it was about?

Ricky: [losing his certainty again] Yeah. She's usually said she's tired.

Therapist: How come you think she's lying to you?

Pause. This is a very challenging, confrontational question; but on the other hand, she is on his side because basically that's what he's trying to say. It is a thinking question, and good for him to reflect on.

Ricky: [Puts his head in his hands, his elbows on his knees, looking down at the floor. This brings up some very sad memories for him.] Because that's how women are. My own mother was that way. H---l, if my own mother lied to me, then why should I believe any woman?

Therapist: [gently] That was painful. How did she lie?

Ricky: After my father left, my mother wanted to get rid of me. That's the truth. I don't need a shrink to tell me that wasn't the case. There was nothing holding her to me at that point. She would leave me with her sister's family or an aunt. I was shuffled from one person to another. One person or another who was too busy for me. They didn't have a word for me. And my mother just told me she was "busy." What a liar!

Therapist: Wow. So, basically, you were an abandoned, neglected child. [She lets the truth of this statement hang in the air for a while.]

Pause. This, truly, is his trauma. His father *and* his mother abandoned him. He believed that the women in his life, his mom and his aunt, were lying. He hoped marriage would be different, but his original neglect led him to believe the worst of women. So he set himself up for unhappiness. By naming the wounds he received, it makes it possible for the therapist and Ricky to return to the concept in the future. It also takes a little of the sting out by bringing it into the open. Finally, it is a very compassionate statement from her; it lets him know that she knows exactly what he went through.

Ricky: Yeah.

Therapist: Now it makes sense to me why you would just assume women would neglect and abandon you. Reject you. Now it really makes sense.

Pause. On the one hand, the therapist is very empathetic; but on the other hand, she is paving the way to refute his concept. It makes sense given his history, but history needn't dictate the future.

[Ricky is silent.]

Therapist: Do you suppose every woman in the world feels like that?

Ricky: I'm not married to every woman in the world.

Therapist: Well, your wife chose you. She married you. How is that a form of abandonment and rejection?

[Now Ricky is a little confused. Good. That's the idea.]

Ricky: Well, that isn't. But later on . . .

Therapist: Was there anything she ever did before the baby came that made you feel abandoned or rejected?

Ricky: [thoughtful] No, I don't remember anything like that.

Therapist: Hmm. So, up till then, you felt good about how your wife felt about you.

Ricky: Yes, actually. We were very much in love.

Pause. At this point, the therapist can introduce her concept. He has been shown alternate ways of seeing their relationship and now may be open to considering new ideas.

Therapist: Here's what I think. Do you want to hear it?

Ricky: Yes.

Therapist: I think you are so used to thinking women—people—will abandon and reject you because of the awful time you had growing up—a very, very painful childhood—that when something feels uncomfortable, you automatically put that negative spin on it.

Ricky: Well, but, it seemed . . . You don't think she rejected me?

Therapist: No. I think she was tired. Like she said.

Ricky looks kind of dazed. He can see how he could have taken something simple and made it unnecessarily complex in his own mind. The session is pretty much over, and he gets up to leave.

Could an accomplishment like this have occurred without therapy? I think about that question a lot. It's awfully hard to see yourself from a more objective position. I'm hoping that readers will find that they can use this book to get past those obstacles that we humans create for ourselves. However, if that objective third party would help, *go for it.* There's no shame in getting an expert opinion. [Please see my website for additional resources: www.TheHealingIsMutual.com]

Once Ricky comes to realize that his wife was only tired and nothing more, he can see that his own behavior was nasty and cold. He has to let this sink in for a while in order to be ready to accept responsibility. Unlike TV, this doesn't happen one-two-three. Sometimes, in therapy, it's ten sessions, sometimes six months. It is rare that a person sees the light in one visit. But it does happen.

The therapist had two jobs to do with Ricky. The first was to get him to see that because he was wounded in childhood, he may have been playing victim in his marriage. That is, he may have jumped to the incorrect assumption that his wife was rejecting him, when she actually was just tired. This was accomplished in this visit.

The second job was to help Ricky to realize that he mistreated Jean. Of course, he recognized that the insult he gave his wife in the restaurant was an example of a put-down. However, it is important for him to see that that was not the beginning of his unkindness.

What was the first thing he did that was destructive? His withdrawal from Jean when she needed him most. His withdrawal was both physical since he didn't help with the childcare, and emotional because he acted cold. Withdrawal is emotional abandonment. Isn't it funny how he was guilty of the one thing that wounded him the most? You would think that because that injured him so much, he'd be really careful not to do it himself, but no, that's not what happens. People often do as was done to them.

Deb Schwarz Hirschhorn, Ph.D.

At their next visit, the therapist questioned Ricky on how the problem started:

Therapist: So, did you have any further thoughts this week about how your relationship took a nose-dive?

Ricky: I've been kicking myself all week. I feel awful. And I've been yelling at Jean more. Not because she deserves it. She doesn't. I see that. But I'm in such a bad, bad mood. Things are worse. Terrible.

Pause. Unfortunately, this is exactly what child neglect or other mistreatment does to the person and why I say that adults who were injured as children must heal. Ricky is blaming, blaming, blaming. And most of that blame is going to himself. Because he feels so miserable with himself now that he realizes that Jean didn't deserve any of what he did, he is more likely to be grumpy. He takes it out on Jean because that's what people do who feel miserable. This will be a challenge for the therapist.

Therapist: Oh, that's bad. Tell me why you are so angry at yourself.

Ricky: I just got real clear that I was expecting to be treated badly, so when she was tired, I figured she was rejecting me. When you pointed that out last week, I hated myself. And I could not stop being disgusting to her.

Therapist: Ricky, it's wonderful that you see it. It's really important to know when someone is trying to hurt you as opposed to when you're seeing something that's not there. Do you suppose Jean hates you now?

Ricky: For some reason, she doesn't. She hasn't spoken to me much, but there's been no hostility from her end. I would think she'd want to leave me.

Therapist: Can you see that that is your theme of abandonment playing again?

Ricky: Yeah, you're right.

Therapist: How about checking out how she feels? Why don't you just ask her? And no more bad behavior to her, okay?

Honesty is the foundation of trust-building.

(Tool 102) Reflect on This . . .

Can you see where your own behavior has been hurtful—and wrong? Can you explain why? Now that you read the above, do you see it more clearly?

Here the therapist is attempting to bring some reality into the picture. Ricky's self-hate will diminish somewhat if he believes Jean does not hate him. Notice the therapist is not pounding him at this time for his continued mistreatment. That would only increase his self-hate and bad behavior.

3. Hate What You've Done but Love Yourself

You must not hate yourself. It's important to recognize that you made a mistake because you weren't brought up by people who could teach you the right way to treat people. You goofed, yes. But don't go hating yourself because if you do that, what happens? It will bring you—and your partner—more pain and I think you've both had enough.

So, how do you hate the act and not the actor? I once had a client who was a recovering alcoholic who said, "I'd rather die than take a drop of alcohol." I was scared she would commit suicide if something bad came up. But I was wrong. She was making a statement that she would hate the *act* of taking that drink so much that she would have to be tested with a choice of death. Thankfully, she was never faced with that test, and it is now sixteen years since she made that statement to me—and stayed clean, sober, and living her life.

Clearly, one part of this process has to be to start loving yourself. It is important to have clear in your mind what about you is good. It is important to see inside your own heart and love what you see. You need to counterbalance the negative messages coming from your past and from yourself. Below are three steps to loving yourself.

You need plenty of positive to counteract the negative you grew up with. I want you to make an *exhaustive* list of all your positive qualities.

A balanced view of yourself is an accurate view—and a healthy one.

(Tool 103) How to Value & Love Yourself #1
Make a list of "My good points." List all your talents, skills, accomplishments, personality qualities, attitudes, values, etc. that should go in here. Don't give lip service to the homework. It's got to come from the heart and soul. If it doesn't, it isn't real and it won't stick.

The next step—after *several weeks* of this work—is to begin to focus on what you did that was wrong. I do not want you to make excuses for yourself; however, it will be necessary to scientifically understand what led up to the bad behavior. For example, in the criminal justice system, when a criminal has been found guilty of a crime, there is a sentencing hearing. The lawyer for the criminal can then introduce mitigating circumstances. Mitigating circumstances are things that happened to the criminal so as to show the forces acting on him. This can include his own emotional injury, being in war, other trauma, even having been hit by a car and suffering brain injury.

Mind you: None of these mitigating circumstances takes away from his guilt. They are meant to take away, a little, from the severity of the sentence. Sometimes mitigating circumstances can even make the difference between a convicted murderer getting the death penalty or getting life in prison.

I'm asking you to do the same thing for yourself. I'm asking you to reflect on your whole life and understand what mitigating circumstances may have led you to behave as you did.

Flexibility is the ability to look objectively at your behavior.

(Tool 104) How to Love & Value Yourself #2
Go back to the autobiography you began in Chapter One. Using the knowledge you have acquired in Part II and especially in this chapter, take a good look at the influences on your behavior and fill in gaps.

Now is the time to closely examine the offending behavior. You are now fortified with a lot on your side: You should have positive feelings about yourself from doing Step 1. You should have a scientific awareness of how you went down the path that you did from doing Step 2. Now is the time to examine the damage you have done *as behaviors*. They are behaviors; they are not you. Do you see the difference? The only people who cannot do this exercise would be truly evil people. Anyone who would not want to mistreat their partner can and should successfully do this exercise.

Ricky did do his homework assignment. He was awfully scared to get the rejection that he believed was coming. But for some reason, his counselor's understanding gave him courage. He realized that he had suffered greatly, which would lead him to automatically think he was going to be mistreated again. He realized that this experience and way of thinking was responsible for his coldness to Jean and his subsequent anger. He asked Jean if she hated him. She was genuinely stunned at his question. She looked at him blankly. "Why am I still here if I hated you?" she asked. "Don't you think a lot of people have told me to leave? But I didn't, did I?" Now Ricky is puzzled. "Well, how could you love a no good

Deb Schwarz Hirschhorn, Ph.D.

b-----d like me?" he blurted out.

Jean's warm heart, which is what he fell in love with, reached out to him. Her protective instincts held her back. She didn't want to go around this path another time in the future, and she was afraid that if she just reached out to him, it would be like sweeping the dust under the rug. She took a deep breath. "I don't know how," was the best compromise she could come up with, not a denial that she still loved him, and not an admission either. They stared at each other for a while. "I—I'm sorry," Ricky stammered. "I'm so sorry I hurt you." He put his head in his hands and started to cry. His crying made Jean angry. She figured he should be feeling sorry for her after what he put her through, not for himself. But she didn't say anything. The apology was a good start. The new attitude and awareness was a good start.

Now is the time to recognize that you have a soul. Begin to honor it.

(Tool 105) How to Love & Value Yourself #3
Clarify in your mind the difference between bad behavior and a bad self. Reject the behavior, not yourself. Please explain this in your own words.

---

4. Resolving Never to Do it Again, No Matter What

There are three tools in this section. The first one is to figure out a way to respond differently the next time you are presented with the same sort of situation that has provoked bad behavior in the past. It must be something that will block the usual response from occurring. You might call this "Heading off Misdeeds at the Pass." Tool 64 to bite your tongue is one such example.

Ginger knows that when she gets home from work, the house will be a mess. She also knows that Gregg has worked hard and just because he gets home one hour earlier does not necessarily give him time to get

162

the kids to pick up their toys. Yet, somehow, without fail, if she walks in and sees the mess, she explodes. Although she has learned to keep her frustration to herself, the stress is still there. Ginger and Gregg put their heads together as a team and decided that (a) Given how hard Ginger works, she should not have to come in and see that chaos which is so demoralizing; (b) Given how hard Gregg works, he can be forgiven if he needs some personal time to unwind. So, they offered the babysitter an extra half hour of time to pick up after the children and wash the day's dishes. Sure, it will be great when Ginger gets control of her temper, but why tempt her when an easy solution can not only avoid the blowup, but make her feel less stressed?

Ralph knows that if he asks Sandy for sex and she says, "No," he will feel rejected. He has been working on expressing his bad feelings before blowing up. Still, it would be nice not to be hurt at all. He sat down with Sandy as a team to discuss why she so frequently refuses him. He told her it makes him feel ugly and awful. She explained that when he says something nasty to her, blames her, criticizes, or makes her feel put down, it takes her about three weeks to forget and then forgive. In the meantime, she doesn't want anything to do with him. She understands he is really working hard on himself now and wants to have the beautiful relationship they once had, but that three weeks—combined with him returning to being fun-loving and nice—is what it will take for her to heal. He decided to mark the calendar the next time he backslides in his work on himself so he can time the three weeks of good behavior.

Planning for the inevitable may avoid the inevitable.

(Tool 106) How to Never do it Again #1
Review all the times you were hurtful in the last several weeks. Get clear on what may have precipitated it and plan ways to block yourself from doing it again.

It's also important to recognize that it is human to backslide, especially under stress. I wouldn't expect Ricky to never lose his temper again.

That's why it's also critically necessary to be prepared.

There are *physical* activities like time out, deep breathing, and relaxation, and *mental* activities like overcoming victim thinking which must be started immediately after you begin to backslide so that you can catch it before it gets worse. If you're lucky, your partner won't even know that you almost slipped.

That is, the more you use these tools, the better you will be able to recover from a fumble.

Use your tools when you slip and keep depression at bay.

```
(Tool 107) How to Never do it Again #2
Post sticky notes all around or program your phone to remind
you which tools to use to recover should you fumble. Log
them to see which ones work best.
```

If you backslide frequently, perhaps there is an *emotional obstacle* to really committing to rid your heart—and behavior—of aggression. The most common obstacle is addiction to relief. Let me explain.

You want to avoid pain. So it really feels good when it stops. When something really feels good, you run the risk of becoming addicted to it. For example, it is statistically a fact that more alcoholics were emotionally abused than were not. They were hurting. They drank. The drinking stopped the constant ache, which felt wonderful, so they became addicted. The alcohol itself is a chemical addiction but the relief from painful thoughts is also a chemical addiction. That is why excessive shopping, gambling, and being a workaholic accomplish the same chemical changes in the brain. When you are not re-experiencing a painful aspect of your life, the brain chemistry is different than when you are.

Here's another point: the more injurious the life lived, the more addictive the "substance."

You can see that you don't need a chemical "substance" to cause a chemical addiction. Let's say you feel badly and the way you "relieve" that feeling is to blow up. Blowing up discharges energy. The fatigue that results after a knock-down drag-out fight is calming, relaxing. The chemicals in your brain have actually changed. And you can get addicted to that.

Once you realize this, you must overcome your addiction just as if you were addicted to cocaine. Step by step, day by day, with hope, a lot of effort in following all the suggestions in this book, and by catching yourself as it's happening if not before.

Not giving in to what's bad makes you stronger—even if it is difficult.

(Tool 108) How to Never do it Again #3
If you enjoy the calm feeling after a blow-up—that is a sign of addiction. You must make extra effort to use the calming techniques in this book in place of the blowups.

---

5. A Review on Overcoming Victim Thinking

Playing victim can lead to aggression.

Nathaniel Brazill was an honor student and a hard worker from an African American family. Barry Grunow, a previous teacher of the year, was his favorite teacher. Brazill had been sent home on the last day of school for playing with water balloons. He was furious because this meant he couldn't say goodbye for the summer to Dinora Rosales, his first girlfriend and with whom he had recently shared his first kiss. He returned to school with a gun and stood in front of Mr. Grunow's class, demanding to speak to Dinora. When Mr. Grunow told him he could not interrupt his class, he pulled out his gun and fired. So, at the age of thirteen, Brazill was tried for murder and found guilty.[1]

In the newspaper account, Brazill stated that he wanted then, and still wants now, to be thought of as a good person. He said, "I try to have faith that if I do the right thing, it will matter." He has formed a prison Gospel choir that performs each Sunday. He obtained his high school diploma and took a correspondence course in legal research, which he uses to help other inmates. He apologized to his mother for the fact that it's a four-hour trip for her to visit, and he warned his younger brother to stay away from violent video games.[2] If he weren't in prison for murder, you'd think he was a Boy Scout.

Before he allowed his anger and his emotions to rule him, Brazill most definitely thought like a victim. Here's what another newspaper account said: "He was a playful, smart kid who dreamed of being a hero to those he admired. At the top of his list were his mother, the president of the United States, and a little girl at school. . . . He made a drawing of a house he designed for his mother, Polly Powell, and the girl he liked at school, Dinora Rosales, studding the yard in the drawing with land mines to protect them. He played kill-the-enemy computer games and watched save-America movies, dreaming of single-handedly rescuing the world from evil. He even wrote to the president, saying he wanted to serve and protect him in the Secret Service. And he swiped a gun from a family friend to learn how to shoot, to prepare for a life of protecting people.[3]

Where did all this start? We have a clue from an interview his mother, Polly Powell gave. According to Time magazine, she claimed that "he was surrounded by domestic abuse and alcoholism at home. She never made good choices in men, she said. The cops had gone to the family's house five times on domestic violence calls."[4]

Children dream of being heroes, but how many create dream homes that are protected all around with land mines? And how many actually steal a gun and learn to use it so as to one day be able to protect the president? Bottom line is that underneath the bravado of many kids is cold fear. Fear clearly was operating in Brazill's attitude and approach to life. Everyone was an enemy, or a potential enemy. He loved Mr. Grunow; he would never have killed him . . . except at the moment that Mr. Grunow felt to him like The Enemy.

Inevitably, if you see yourself as mistreated, you may come to attack others in self-defense.

I was talking to a couple about their eight-year-old daughter. The child kept staining her clothes, and the mother was sending her to school that way because they were poor and it was really hard for her to put together the money for more uniform shirts. As we talked, the mother unexpectedly blurted out, "Why does everyone get clothes before me? Why do I have to go around like a rag picker in these clothes so I can buy my husband a $300 suit to look good for work?" I asked her whom she was angry at. I thought maybe she was angry at me, which would have been the logical choice since I was the one that insisted the child have fresh clothes, but no, these things are not logical. Her answer, turning to her husband, was, "At him! And at my daughter!" She remained quite indignant, and finally had to leave the room.

Now, we had been working on being mindful of not playing victim. This family had put yellow sticky notes all over the house reminding them to watch for episodes like this one. When the mother returned, I challenged her, saying, "So if you want to spend money on clothes for yourself and you feel you can't stand it any more, is your daughter stopping you?"

Of course, she replied, "No." Then I asked, "Whose idea was it that your husband should have the nice suit for work?" Letting out a deep sigh, she said, "Mine." "So," I responded, "how can you blame them for your choices?" "I guess," she admitted in a small voice, "I was playing victim."

How easy it is to fall into that trap. It will take lots of work to get out of it, but that's okay. That work takes you in the right direction.

Remove the shackles of victim thinking once and for all.

(Review Tools 5-11) Reflect on This . . .

What triggers you into victim thinking? What do you think
triggers your partner into it? What can you do to prevent it?
What can you do once you're in it? How can you help your
partner when he is in it? Is there something you would like
your partner to do for you when you are in it? Can you tell
him?

Chapter Thirteen
Six Things to Keep in Mind

Before we close Part II, I'd like to review some of the points that resonate the most for me.

1. Abusers Were Victims

People who were maltreated as children are likely to grow up to either be mistreated in their relationships or to *believe* they are being mistreated in those relationships because that is what is familiar to them [Refer to p. 5, Chapter One].

The only exception to that turns out not to be an exception at all. That happens when a parent lets a child get away with misbehavior.

Melanie [Refer to p. 14] *kept shaking her head at the idea that her husband thought she was putting him down by inquiring about his pay raise. She had to keep reminding herself, "He was really badly abused as a child." Doing that gave her patience when he would backslide into victim thinking.*

Doesn't it feel good to be ahead of the game now that you've been using the tools?

(Tool 109) Reflect on This . . .
Can you see how you or your partner (or both) were victims? Can you see how you (or both) need to heal? Which healing tools from this book do you like best?

---

2. Being Maltreated Is Traumatic—So Be Patient with the Healing

Being told again and again "you're stupid" by someone who is supposed to love you is traumatic [Refer to p. 87]. Trauma does not have to happen all at once. In fact, the most difficult trauma to shake is the kind that lasts and lasts. It is so familiar it seems as though it's normal. In the medical world, "trauma" means injury. Injury means there's something not functioning right; there's a wound. Therefore, an adult with a traumatic childhood can't easily "get over it."

Marla [Refer to p. 83] *was so used to being dismissive of her husband, Bob, that it didn't even occur to her to look at herself and notice that her behavior was cruel and pointless. Bob had had it. "I can't take the pain anymore," he said, and Marla could feel herself starting to mimic his pain: "Can't take it anymore." But Bob continued, "so I want a divorce." That was a splash of cold water in her face. The next day, Marla made an appointment for counseling.*

Marla: There's something wrong with me. I'm a very sick woman. My first impulse is always to put him down. But I love Bob. Why do I treat him so badly? Why do I want to make fun of him, even his pain?

Therapist: I suspect some trauma in your own life.

A far-away look crossed Marla's face. A long-buried memory popped up.

Marla: I was fourteen. My mother and I had been shopping for a dress because I had been invited to the junior prom. When my father saw me dressed up, he spat out, "Slut!" I kept asking my mom, "What does he mean?" I really didn't know. And she said, "Don't worry about it."

Therapist: Was that how your relationship with him always went?

Marla: Pretty much. He didn't have anything positive to say. For him, positive was just not making mean remarks. If he bought my sister a dress, he didn't buy one for me. I don't know why. He just favored her. If I went into their room, let's say to talk to my mother, he would slam the door in my face.

Therapist: Was your mom protective?

Marla: Not really. She was either getting ready to go to work, or sleeping from being tired from work. I think she kind of tried to stand up for us, but she coulda done more. Finally she left my father; we moved to a better apartment and I was relieved to not see him anymore. But that didn't last. He joined us not much later; I don't remember why. I started running away. I was hoping my mom would come look for me but she never did.

Therapist: How did you deal with that?

Marla: I shut down. I don't think about it. I just remembered it because of what you said.

Therapist: Sure. Who'd want to remember something like that? Were there any good memories of your childhood?

Marla: No, I can't think of any.

Therapist: What life rule did you take away from your childhood?

Marla (thoughtful): Somebody is going to make you feel like garbage sooner or later.

Therapist: Does your husband make you feel like garbage?

Marla: No, he is a good man. I just can't stand how weak he is! That's why I give it to him; it drives me crazy.

The therapist did not ask Marla to explain herself; she wouldn't have been able to. What she is saying is that she is afraid of life because it is a jungle. Her husband, who is a gentle soul, is unprepared for this jungle. This scares her and enrages her. By being "weak," he cannot protect her. Not only is she guilty of victim thinking but she is living in a state of constant trauma. She lives as though she is in a war zone.

The therapist suggested a session with Bob who reluctantly came in. The therapist explained to Bob that due to his wife's childhood abuse, she will need time to heal. He might not see much improvement for three to six months. She asked him to hang in there before going ahead with the divorce, and he reluctantly agreed.

During that time, Bob was to come in as well to learn how to stand up to Marla effectively and non-aggressively and to heal himself.

Progress, however, came sooner than he or the therapist expected.

Understanding that abuse is trauma will give you patience through this difficult process.

> ### (Tool 110) Reflect on This . . .
> Can you see how your maltreatment was traumatic for you or your partner or both? Explain trauma and how that will, on a very practical level, affect your relationship.

3. The Vast, Overwhelming Majority of Abusers Are Not Mean, Nasty, Hateful People.

Yes, there definitely are some bad apples, but most people whose behavior is cruel do not mean to be mean [Refer to p. 126, footnote 1, Gottman research]. They don't know how to handle their bad feelings and anger. That means it's important not to give up on abusers. They may really want to change. First of all, they are unhappy from their childhood experience, and second, they are unhappy with themselves.

Hearing Bob's agreement to hold off on the divorce, Marla started crying. Bob had never seen her cry before.

<u>Marla</u>: Oh, thank you. I'm so sorry for everything. So very, very sorry.

This in no way could make up for years of tormenting him, but it was a beginning.

It's easier to assist others to change behavior when you can see that their souls are good.

(Tool 111) Reflect on This . . .

Are you and your partner good people? Can you put the bad behavior aside for a moment and get a clear view of your partner or yourself?

---

4. Anger Is a Survival Instinct

Bob was suffering and his wife's therapist was asking him to hang in. What a rotten place to be. He didn't understand why he was being mistreated. He wondered why Marla didn't have another way of expressing frustration or disappointment or sadness or feelings of abandonment or rejection. After all, logic dictates that if she felt rejected and didn't want to feel that way, she'd go out of her way to act nice so as not to be rejected again. But logic doesn't rule, emotions do. And the emotion of anger and the behavior of sarcasm were learned as protective mechanisms [Refer to p. 5].

Given that her parents were rejecting, she learned that she couldn't be nice so as to win them over. "Nice" wouldn't work. What's left? Well, anger is a good one. It's scary, so it keeps nasty people away; it's protective.

This is not to justify anger. It is only to understand where it comes from—to understand that it is not personal; it's a behavioral choice where no other choice existed. Bob didn't deserve the anger and neither did you, and if you were to ask your partner in a moment of peace and quiet between you, your partner would tell you that. The good part about this is that it is correctable. Correction requires willingness to learn new ways and a recognition that anger backfires. Marla will have to work hard with her tools.

After he got home from his visit to the therapist, Bob was more confused than ever. He decided to deal directly with Marla.

<u>Bob</u>: *I just have a question. Why did you mistreat me? Why did you get angry at everything I did?*

<u>Marla</u>: *You know, that's a good question. I don't even know why. You don't deserve it. You're a good man. I was on automatic pilot, reacting.*

5. Hurt People Can Be Highly Sensitive

Hurt people can be highly sensitive, so be careful as you start to open the doors of communication. Think before you speak. Frequently offenders are sensitive only to themselves, not necessarily to their long-suffering spouses [Refer to p. 81, Tool 48]. Being sensitive to oneself is a great beginning. Cold-hearted people are neither sensitive to themselves nor to others. It makes sense that a mistreated person—if he didn't learn to be numb to avoid pain—would be extra sensitive to his own feelings.

Answering the next two questions will show you what you have mastered so far—and that will feel quite good.

(Tool 112) Explain This . . .
When Ricky was hurt because Jean did not want sex with him after Goldie arrived, was that sensitivity? To whom?

(Tool 113) Explain This . . .
When Jean was painting the living room and left him out, was Ricky's reaction one of sensitivity? To whom?

[Answers: 112 — No. That was a misinterpretation of Jean's behavior. In other words, it was playing victim.

174

113 – Yes. His being hurt was attributed to the reality that she left him out. He was sensitive to himself.]

Sometimes power comes from being sensitive.

(Review Tools 46-49) Reflect on This . . .
Are you sensitive or insensitive? What about your partner? What caused that? How will you work on that . . . together?

---

6. Give your partner the benefit of the doubt

Don't assume your partner meant badly or your efforts are squashed before they start. (We're talking here about mildly unpleasant words; we are NOT talking about obvious verbal or physical attack.)

One night a noise woke me up. My husband and I went to investigate and our talking was louder in the silence of the night than we realized. We accidentally woke up our son, who was 18 at the time. He not only did not yell at us, he didn't even assume that we did it unlovingly. Could we have been quieter? Certainly. But we made an error in judgment rather than being carelessly inconsiderate, and he understood that.

Make just this one tool part of your life and you will rebuild trust.

(Review Tool 14) Reflect on This . . .
How will you switch your thinking around to give your partner the benefit of the doubt?

PART III

Empowering Yourself

The abuse has stopped. Now what? Part III is about yourself – and that's not selfish. To create a new marriage, you have to feel good inside. Some of that will come from the care and kindness that your partner is starting to show you. Some of that will come from the tools in Part IV for rebuilding your relationship. But some of that must come from self-healing. That's what Part III is about.

Chapter Fourteen
Eight Healing Activities for Your "Self"

Many people feel like they have lost themselves during their marriage. Getting rid of bad behavior creates a space in which to build something positive and happy. That "something" begins with yourself. Chapter 14 is about finding, nurturing and affirming your Self.

1. Get re-acquainted with yourself

How can a person be so out of contact with herself that she doesn't even know who she is? It may begin in childhood.

Imagine a small child sitting in a high chair being fed. Mom wants that child to eat. Eating is obviously important, so mom says, "Oh, this is delicious, soooo good." The little child tastes it. Suppose the child spits it out and grins. What should the mom do? Mom should put the food aside, end the meal, and let the little one go play. Why? Because if the child was really hungry, he would have eaten it. The grin indicates a game.

But suppose mom is worried the child hasn't eaten well. Suppose the mom has engaged in a power struggle with her child. (Silly, but common.) So maybe mom gets mad and says, "This is good! You like it! Eat it!" Frightened, the child may eat. Over time, that child gets used to eating things because mom said to, not because the child likes them. Growing up that way, such a child can lose touch with his own tastes. Many people choose professions and marriage partners because that is what their parents wanted.

A young lady of 22 once came to me to ask if she should marry a certain man. Making that decision is not my job. But her parents opposed the marriage and she was so confused that she didn't know what she really felt. Her parents promised her a job and financial security if she just did what they wanted. That young lady lived in a gilded cage from which she didn't even know if she wanted to escape.

Marriage, too, can rob you of your identity. When you have been told what to do and think [Refer to Chapter Four, Power and Voice, p. 41], or you have been belittled [Refer to Chapter Seven, Put-Downs: They're No Joke, p. 83] or you have been scared to express yourself [Refer to Chapter Ten, Scaring into Submission, p. 125], you can, eventually, lose touch with who you are. Now is the time to reconnect with yourself.

Think of knowledge about yourself as divided up into different categories, so one category might be "my opinions about politics," and another might be, "my values in business." Start by selecting one category at a time.

Let's begin with a relatively uncomplicated category, say, clothing. Go to the mall and start by comparing two items. You may not be ready to say, "Oh, wow, I love this and I hate this," but you may be able to reach deep inside and say, "I like this one a little better than this one." What do you like? What don't you like as well about the other? Is it the color? The pattern? The cut? Being dressy versus being casual? The way it's made? The way the pieces go together? The way it blends with your coloring? When you think about your experience, what did you discover about your preferences, values, and opinions that you weren't consciously aware of before?

You can go through this process for lots of categories: food, furniture, politics, friends, landscaping, decorating, jobs, hobbies, the opposite sex, values and so on.

To know yourself is to be strong.

(Tool 114) Getting to Know Myself Checklist	
My tastes & preferences	
Food	
Clothing	
Housing	
Neighborhood	
Free time	
Vacations	
Music	
Art	
Furniture	
Colors	
Books	
Movies	
Computers	
Other equipment	
My values (regarding…)	
Religion	
Having children	
Extended family	
Getting married	
Politics	
War	
Life	

Add various issues, such as abortion, education, dealing with terrorists, corruption, the economy, whatever, and keep adding ideas and areas of value.

Ideals are not impossible, just difficult.

(Tool 115) Reflect on This . . .

1. What do you enjoy doing for down-time?
2. What sort of work would you really like to do if you were free to change what you're doing?
3. What do you wish your partner would say/do to make you happy?
4. Why are you unhappy?

---

2. Do Affirmations

If an insulting parent or a cruel partner or even an offensive boss spent a lot of time drumming a message of worthlessness into you, then you may come to believe it about yourself. We have been calling that "victim thinking." In addition to the tools in Chapter One to change victim thinking [Refer to pp. 7-21], here is another one: Do affirmations. Affirmations are positive messages we say to ourselves about ourselves.[1]

However, given the number of times we have heard the negative message, it takes a lot of repetition of an opposite message to undo it. Neuropsychological research supports this. Similar experiences, when repeated, etch neural pathways in the brain. If those experiences were bad, how do you undo them? The good news is that unused neural pathways will fade out eventually. Therefore, the first step in eliminating victim thinking is to refrain from negative self-talk. By stopping this line of thought, the corresponding neural pathways will fade out.

That's half the battle! Next, we build new pathways through affirmations.

For example, do you remember Lenny who told Lenore she was a klutz [Refer to p. 63]? Although he later read this book and felt great remorse [Refer to pp. 101-102], that really didn't do much for Lenore. Certainly, for her to heal, it's necessary for her to no longer hear these negative messages. But it's not sufficient. New messages need to be put where the old ones were. Not only that, she needs to stop repeating Lenny's negative messages. Lenore can no long think of herself as a klutz, or in more general terms, a screw-up. She will need to make an affirmation such as, "I am a competent person."

This solution, however, poses its own problem: We don't believe the positive statements. So how do we get around that?

Here's the solution: Look for the exception to your rule. If you believe that you are, for example, a wimp, look for the times you weren't and remind yourself of them whenever you talk negatively to yourself.

Amy was nervous; she was going to pick up her husband, Edward, at work— and she was late. If she was late in the past, he would start questioning her: "Where were you?" "Who did you talk to?" and so forth. He no longer does that, but the bad feelings from the past remained. To make matters worse, because she was rushing a police officer pulled her over. She took a deep breath and remembered her relaxation process. Right then, she allowed her body to relax, part by part. "I'm sorry, officer," was all she said. He wrote the ticket and she immediately congratulated herself for not breaking down in tears. "I handled that well," she thought. She continued on to where she was to meet her husband. When she arrived, she smiled at him. He couldn't help but smile back. She proudly told him her story.

Two weeks later, Amy was preparing a talk she needed to give before a committee on which she served. This was the sort of thing that would make her nervous. "I'm such a wimp," she started to say. Then she caught herself and thought, "How dare you talk to me like that! Why just a couple weeks ago I handled that ticket so well. And then I even handled Edward well too. Far from being a wimp, I'm a cool lady who handles stress well."

If you've given space in your head for negative self-talk, it's time to kick it out.

(Tool 116) How to Do Affirmations
Make your affirmations real and believable by looking for the exceptions to the negative rule that you have told yourself. When you say the affirmations, think of those exceptions and be proud of them.

Clean out Abuser Values

Affirming yourself at dark moments is very difficult. You may feel so down or angry that you don't remember to do the affirmations. This is victim thinking at its most devastating. What happened is that you heard unkind judgments about yourself in childhood. What's worse is that you have come to accept these unkind judgments as your own: They *feel* as if they were your own thoughts. These negative beliefs are called *abuser values.*

You see, victim thinking comes from more than having been mistreated in childhood. It also emanates from absorbing abuser values from your parents and unwittingly adopting them.

Sometimes, you may know, objectively, that you are a good person, yet you have an overpowering feeling that you are rotten. If you have experienced this, it means you were brainwashed. Your task now is to recognize abuser values for what they are—foreign thoughts that you must dislodge from your brain.

When negative thoughts are so deeply embedded that it doesn't even occur to you to say your affirmation, you may find yourself sinking into a pit of despair. It is not normal to be down like that. Therefore, an abuser value must be lodged in your head to cause that reaction. It is the abuser value, not anything objective, that led to despair. So it is the abuser value itself that must be routed out.

We are going to use this very pit of despair to help turn everything around.

Next time you find yourself in that pit, use that feeling as a clue to search for the abuser value behind it. Ask yourself: What just happened? Did someone say something that triggered those bad feelings?

Some weeks after Amy's encounter with a traffic cop, she and Edward were at a party. She said hello to someone she had recently met and thought this woman's name was "Sylvia." The lady politely corrected her, "Shelby." Amy wanted to sink into the ground. She mustered up a false smile, said, "Shelby," and moved along with her husband to another cluster of people. When they got home from the event, she was very down. Amy could almost hear her mother's voice saying, "You just can't get things right, can you?"

"I felt so stupid, Edward," Amy told her husband. "I met Shelby there and called her, 'Sylvia.' She corrected me."

Luckily, Edward, who had been working through the book himself, asked her, "Isn't this an example of an abuser value getting in your head?"

"I felt so stupid," she repeated. A far-away look came over her. "My mother always told me I couldn't get anything right. She was right, you see."

"That is so utterly ridiculous," Edward came back. "First of all, such things happen to everyone. Why, I just met someone tonight and when I introduced myself, he said to me, 'Nice to meet you, chap, but you know I won't remember your name!' He didn't even think anything of saying that. And second of all, even if it were a terrible faux-pas, let us just say for a minute it was, does it require this level of self-battery?"

Amy thought long and hard about that. She realized that, indeed, she had an abuser value in control of her head. She smiled and thanked Edward for being there for her. She remembered her affirmation and the traffic cop episode. Thinking of how nicely she handled that, she said aloud, "I'm a cool lady who handles stress well." She added a new one that she realized was absolutely necessary, "I get 90 percent of things right and that's pretty good!"

Watch out for abuser values at the root of depressed moods.

(Tool 117) How to Clean Out Abuser Values
1. When you're feeling down or angry, that may be a clue that an abuser value is running its mouth in your head. Tune in to it.
2. Challenge the truth of it.
3. Create and say an affirmation that contradicts it.

---

3. Surround Yourself with Companions Who Affirm You

One of the beauties of connecting with others is that in choosing your company, you can choose those people who affirm you. Would you rather spend time with a buddy who says you're a good person and boosts your morale or someone you've known for a long time, but who brings you down? The latter person may feel more real because, with a history of mistreatment at home, that's what you're most familiar with. But you can get used to the comfort of the person who affirms you, especially if he is sincere.

To discern good people from toxic people, listen to what they say and don't gloss over slips in their behavior that aren't nice. Don't fall into an old pattern of being attracted to the wrong kind of people.

Expand your ciricle. Take a class; go to religious services; join a gardening club, chess club, repertory theater, band, sports, art guild, poetry circle;

become involved in civic activities; get a second job that gives you an opportunity to express your creative side.

Rosemarie went on a second date with a wonderful man. He obviously liked her, and she found him intelligent, interesting, courteous, and attractive. He wanted a third date, but was leaving for a two-week business trip. As he drove her home, they passed a glittery club. "Now that's a great place. I want to take you there. Don't go there till I get back," he said smiling.

He was being possessive; he had stepped over the line. Telling someone what to do without regard for their own decisions is not affirming. A nice guy would have said he'd like to take her there and leave out the rest. Rosemarie should look elsewhere for her next date.

Batya was wearing her new dress and it looked lovely on her. Jack, her date, took her to his friend's party. As they entered, he saw some old friends. "Just a moment," he said to Batya, waving a finger in the air, and he dashed off. He was, indeed, gone not more than five minutes. The rest of the evening, he was polite and attentive. Is he affirming her? No. That first five minutes killed it. "But," Batya might argue, "he saw some old friends. What should he have done, ignore them?"

Actually, he had a lot of choices:

1. He could take her with him and introduce her as his "date." This doesn't make it look serious so his friends will know it is a new relationship.
2. Wait till the friends see him first and come over, then introduce her as his date.
3. Skip the friends. If they are really that close, he'll get another chance to see them on another day. And they'll understand. Unless they're rude, like he is.

Batya will do better not having another date with this person.

Cheston was in financial difficulties, but he finally landed a job. He came home, feeling tired. No sooner did he walk in the door, then the phone rang. It was his mother. Cheston told her the good news; her response was: "It took you long enough."

You can't get rid of mom, but you can either limit the amount of contact or try to educate her. For example, Cheston could respond by cheerfully saying, "C'mon, mom, say something positive about my job troubles. I know you can do it!" A little humor can deliver an effective message.

Sheila had an uneasy feeling on the way to lunch. She was going to get together with Mary, an old friend. She couldn't pinpoint why she had that uneasy feeling. She put it out of her mind. Over lunch, she started telling Mary about the amazing opportunity at work. It would take some maneuvering to be recognized, and if she succeeded in that, she'd have some big-time juggling to do with babysitting. Nevertheless, the financial reward, not to mention the intellectual challenge and responsibility, seemed well worth trying for it. Mary smiled at her, "There you go, Sheila, always stretching out to the stars, to the impossible. And with the stress on your marriage as it is, I really think you ought to get realistic." At that moment, Sheila knew why she'd felt uneasy: Mary always shot down her ideas. Sheila sighed. She realized that nothing she could say would open Mary's eyes to her own negativity. She decided to go for the job opportunity—and to change friends.

You need ammunition to fight abuser values. That's what friends are for.

(Tool 118) How to tell if a friend/family member is not affirming

1. Listen to your gut.
2. Remember that small signs count.

Make a table something like this for yourself:

Doing a clean sweep can be so refreshing.

(Tool 119) Reflect on This…		
List of friends, coworkers, family	Is he affirming of me?	What does she do?
Sue		
Etc.		

What if the person who does not affirm you is your partner? My answer is tell her. At some point along the way, your partner has got to become your real partner.

4. Nurture Your Body and Spirit

You can also affirm yourself through how you treat yourself. Do you take as much care of yourself as you do of other people?

Doris prides herself on being a devoted parent, and she tries to be a good wife. But clearly, she suffers from what so many other women and even some men suffer from—being so good at taking care of everyone else that she shortchanges herself. She decided to add a simple ritual to her day at 4 p.m., precisely the moment she always feels tired: a cup of tea. For her, this was a big step.

It is also necessary to enjoy your work. If you don't, you're either (a) in the wrong profession, (b) in the wrong *office*, (c) working above/below your real level, or (d) just plain not following your heart in some other way. If you absolutely can't switch and you are unhappy, all the more reason to inject goodness in the rest of your life. That's what Cameron and Sharon did.

In the corporate world, Cameron has a demanding job. That's part of what makes him so angry at his wife, Sharon. Because there are four children at home, all under school age, there's no way she can work outside the home. He knows his anger is ridiculous and he's trying to change. Cameron and Sharon both decided to add some nurturing to their lives: Every Wednesday evening they have a friend babysit while they go together to get massages. They reciprocate on Monday, together.

Self-empowerment means taking action.

(Tool 120) Checklist for nurturing yourself:

➢ A walk in the woods, along the beach, or through city streets
➢ A visit to the library or bookstore
➢ Writing for the local paper
➢ A sport
➢ Taking up a hobby (here are some)
- ✓ Astronomy
- ✓ Painting
- ✓ Ceramics
- ✓ Quilting
- ✓ Gardening
- ✓ Guitar
- ✓ Chorus
- ✓ Acting
➢ Getting a pet
➢ Keeping a blog
➢ Joining a club
➢ Listening to and/or playing music you enjoy
➢ Having flowers around
➢ Burning incense or using cedar chips or other aromatic things
➢ Having a fish tank or waterfall for auditory and visual comfort
➢ Fixing up your surroundings so they are visually pleasing to you.

What ideas did this list give you that you'd like to incorporate?

Here's something I do: I start my day with a muffin recipe that I created. I just love that recipe! Nice cup of coffee with it.

When you balance giving to others with giving to yourself, you end up with a whole new appreciation for that Self.

(Tool 121) Reflect on This . . .

The more you meet your own needs, the happier you will be. Do you eat three good meals? Do you work in a pleasant environment? Do you get a good night's sleep? Do you take time for reflection and relaxation, have decent clothes that look good on you, take a daily shower or bath that you stay in long enough to enjoy, have adequate time in the bathroom, keep a comfortable temperature in the house? Do you get fresh air and exercise? These are just the basics. How do you nurture yourself? What else can you do?

List the ways you can create a nurturing environment:

Get organized about being nice to yourself. Keep a checklist:

(Tool 122) Checklist		
Food	Clothing	Sleep
Exercise	Furniture	Friends
Music	Flowers	Shower
Room temperature	Visually pleasing home	Pleasant work environment
Time to think	Time to relax	Reasonable schedule
other		

5. Learn about the Way Others Live

One way of correcting abuser values and reinforcing affirmations is through socializing just to be an observer. Getting to know new people and how they think could be enormously beneficial. Thus, you might go out of your way to connect with someone at work or at your volunteer organization whom you don't feel you have something in common with, just to learn and understand about people. Maybe that person is poor and been struggling financially, yet happy; maybe that person has a loving family and you never did; maybe that person is more talented than you think you are—or less so. It doesn't matter. Get to know a variety of people and try to understand how they think.

Expanding the people in your world is a powerful boost to affirmations.

(Tool 123) Reflect on This . . .
Who can you get to know better? Where would you begin to meet people from whom you can learn what healthy relationships are like?

---

6. Make Meaning of Your Existence

When you are clear on the Big Picture of your life, it becomes easier to do affirmations, it strengthens the fight against abuser values, and it backs you up in picking better friends. So I am asking you to begin a spiritual quest. Spend some time thinking about some of the Big Questions: Why was I born? Why was I created? What is my purpose here on Earth? Where does happiness come in? Is there room for me to be happy?

It seems to me that our Declaration of Independence said it best: It is our job to *pursue* happiness. It's not handed to us on a silver platter, but we have the freedom to go after it. We have to consider the possibility that happiness is attainable and that we, personally, were meant to have it. How can we create meaning and happiness while working on a difficult marriage?

People who say that life has no meaning are nihilists looking to be unhappy.

(Tool 124) Reflect on This . . .

Why were you born? What is the purpose of your life? Is there any logical reason why you should not be able to pursue happiness in your life?

---

7. Give of Yourself to Those in Need

When we give, we feel better. Giving to others affirms the best about ourselves. It is also a way of connecting to others and seeing how other volunteers think and handle life. It is another avenue for using Tool 123 [Refer to p. 192].

Sometimes that giving is very difficult because we hardly have the resources for ourselves. Yet, if we try, giving can come back to us big time.

Figure out where to start by calling your county or city volunteer associations and asking for the names of others. Be a hospital volunteer, animal shelter volunteer, school volunteer, or work with the abuse hotline (only when you are ready). Work with your church, synagogue, or mosque; the county library; the local symphony; environmental groups; teach computer basics to elderly shut-ins. There are directories in every county of this country with enormous listings of places to volunteer. You will gain from helping, and you will gain from the camaraderie with the other helpers.

Giving of yourself gives to yourself.

(Tool 125) Reflect on This . . .

What sort of volunteer work would you find meaningful? How can you make time for it?

---

8. Inject hope into your life

In order to resolve the stickiest of matters, reaching out and talking about it requires the belief that things can get better. Without that, there is no incentive to try. How do you have hope when things look so bad?

Now may be a good time to take a personal inventory of changes that have taken place since you and your partner started working through this book. What do you see different in yourself? What new attitudes do you have? What new skills do you have? What personality qualities do you see improved? For example, are you more patient? Are you less easily stressed? Do you recognize the dynamics of your partner and how those affected her behavior?

Has your partner changed in any way? Can you point to even the littlest things? For example, if the only difference is that she no longer reads the paper while you are supposed to be visiting at breakfast, then that is a step in the right direction. Go through the book and through the notes you've made for all the exercises and see what you notice that is better both on your part and your partner's.

Hope makes everything possible.

(Tool 126) Reflect on This . . .
Make a list of the behaviors and attitudes, both on your part and that of your partner, that are better now. Open the door to let in hope.

Chapter Fifteen
Laughing Is Better than Crying

My daughter and her husband were diligently working on changing their newborn boy's diaper. Suddenly, without warning—there is never warning—the baby took aim, and in seconds, they both got squirted. "We just cracked up," she told me. They thought it was funny. But they got wet! How did they think it was funny, I wanted to know. "Yeah," she said, "if it was somebody else's baby, I probably would have been grossed out. But everything my baby does is cute! We just thought it was funny. So we cleaned him up, put him down, and then got ourselves cleaned up."

Laughing *together* brings a couple together. Let's say for argument's sake that my daughter was annoyed at her husband about something at the time of the diapering event. By letting go of the petty annoyance and laughing instead, she created an opportunity for herself and her husband to enjoy being together. Do you sometimes hold onto an irritation even when you have the opportunity to lighten up instead?

I have been at homes of mourners who, instead of crying at the loss of a loved one, laugh as they remembered his idiosyncrasies or the delightful moments of her life. I marvel at playwrights who find humor in themes such as war and sickness and just about every pox on mankind.

How does a person do that? How does a person somehow convert a serious thing into humor? How does a person see the funny side of the worst things? I have come to the conclusion that being able to see the light side of life is just a good habit. To create the good habit of laughing, we need to give ourselves up to laughter where we didn't previously. It's a matter of letting go.

I was a very serious person growing up. That's because my parents were serious. They bought the New York Times on Sunday and thought papers that carried the comics were silly. Then I met my husband who knew how

195

to laugh. Some of his jokes seemed to me to be just corny and I couldn't bring myself to laugh at them. But I discovered that it feels good to laugh, even if the joke is kind of lame. I just let go and let myself laugh. We had four children and, growing up in a house of silly jokes, they all have the ability to laugh at life.

Cultivate the habit of laughing.

> **(Tool 127) How to Laugh #1**
> Just laugh. It's better than crying. Are you very serious or can you laugh? Can you enjoy other people's humor? Can you find something funny in serious things? Can you let yourself go?

When one of my sons was in first or second grade, he complained that the bigger kids picked on him on the bus. My immediate response to him: Make a joke out of it and that will take the wind out of their sails. It took several years for this to sink in, but it did. Today, he's a funny guy.

See if you can laugh at yourself. Don't be self-deprecating; just recognize your own foibles and laugh.

Have the strength to affirm yourself *and* laugh at yourself.

> **(Tool 128) How to Laugh #2**
> Laugh at your own foibles—in a good-natured way. The more tolerant you are of yourself, the more you will lighten up—and so will everyone around you.

Search for positive outcomes in what appears to be a negative situation. No matter how bad a situation, it is possible to find something positive in it. For example, the grief you feel when a loved one dies is ameliorated by the fond memories of that person, as well as what he stood for that lasts afterwards. In other words, there is always a future—and hope. Then allow these possibilities to bring a smile to your face.

Ricky sat in the therapist's office staring at the floor. He was being asked to find the good that came out of his terrible childhood. He thought the question ridiculous. But the therapist said that there is good in everything. Well, he had to admit that he did learn to function on his own. He had become a responsible adult because of it. He acknowledged that that was good. Nevertheless, he wondered whether his life wouldn't have been better without all that turmoil. Couldn't he have learned responsibility with a normal, loving family?

Then again, the awful episode with his wife, Jean, made him see the meaning of love in a clear, sharp light. He realized that love was not just something you felt but something you did. He had learned to show his love for his wife in a way he would not have been able to do had he not gone through all the previous turmoil. It occurred to him that he actually might possess a deeper sense of what love really is than people who'd had an easier childhood. Interesting, he mused. It brought a smile to his face to think that he might be better off than people who he'd always thought were better off.

Sonny and Vivian were depressed so badly they couldn't focus. Their child had died. It was the most awful experience of their lives. They did not know how they would ever recover. Of course, the truth is, they wouldn't. A parent is never the same after losing a child. Sonny withdrew from Vivian, thinking she was to blame. He started drinking. The house was a chilly place. Several years passed, and they managed to stumble forward in their lives. They had a business and did very well. A friend pointed out that a local boys' school was floundering financially. The school specialized in taking in boys from impoverished homes who probably would have ended on the streets. Instead, the boys in this school won high academic honors in statewide and national competitions. For generations, the school had produced successful men in all walks of life. However, for many reasons, they needed an input of cash and time. Sonny and Vivian refused to get involved, saying, "To see other people's children flourish would just be too hard on us." But their friend kept pressing them, and they reluctantly went to the school to check it out. Their hearts took over. Here were children they could love! They threw themselves into this school as they had never thrown themselves into anything since their child had died. They joined the board; they roped their friends into that board; they got their country club to sponsor golf tournaments. They even volunteered to tutor boys who needed it. They became a team again, and drew closer together. Two decades of boys graduated with honors because of them. Boys wrote them cards at holiday time and came for dinner. Some even called them, "Mom" and "Dad." Many years later, they had to admit that had they not suffered their terrible personal tragedy, they never would have become involved in this school, let alone so involved and committed as they were. Could they smile at their loss? No. But they could smile at the memories of graduation ceremonies in which "their" boys would shine. When they remembered some of the more heartwarming moments, they could even laugh.

It takes courage to see the good when things are bad.

(Tool 129) How to Laugh #3
Search for the positive in every bad thing—it is definitely there. Focus on that for a while and allow a smile to come to your face. Make a list of the bad things that happened in your life and the good that came out of them. How do you feel?

At the other end of the spectrum are people whose obstacles are not tragedies, but they see them that way. Are you one of these people? Your wife overcooked the dinner. So what? You got kept waiting. So what? You were put on hold. So what? Traffic was heavy. So what?

Do these things really matter in the scheme of things? Work hard on stepping back and putting things into proper perspective. While you're doing that, ask yourself how in the world little things got blown out of proportion in your mind. Laugh at the dissonance between what they really are and how you saw them.

Seeing one's tiny place in a big world can actually be very reassuring.

(Tool 130) How to Laugh #4

How important is the problem you're going through, really? Learn to see it in proper proportion—and laugh at how you overrated its significance. List the things that have bothered you about your partner and write down—with honesty— how important they really are.

Here's another way to laugh: Train yourself to think like a comedian. Read the comics. Ask yourself what's funny there. Watch *Seinfeld*. Rent old Eddie Murphy movies. Read books of jokes. Go to humor sites. How is your life like Seinfeld's? Can you see yourself laughing at the same things the comedians do?

Props help in any endeavor.

(Tool 131) How to Laugh #5

Read comics, watch funny movies. Train yourself to see life the way comedians see it. What have you read, seen, or heard lately that is genuinely funny? How can you bring it into your life?

There is, of course, a caveat, and it is a big one. See the chapter on put-downs to understand. The one kind of joke that is FORBIDDEN, totally forbidden, is to laugh at someone else that you are related to. You may laugh at the president. That is permitted. He gets well paid and goes down in history for the privilege of his title, so being the target of jokes is a small price to pay. And you may laugh at yourself because that will take you out of your glum, morose mood. But you may not laugh at those you love or ought to love.

Wilson and Janice had a grueling session. She was totally dissatisfied with Wilson's lackluster attempt at doing the homework that I had assigned him. His homework had been to simply notice what mood Janice was in and just tell her. If he was right, good; if not, she was to help him out a little. The problem was that she was in a bad mood most of the time because (ta da!) of his lack of effort at understanding her moods. And he wasn't doing the work because (ta da!) he didn't want to deal with the bad mood. Finally, at the end of the session, Janice burst into tears. Wilson immediately jumped up, and, pointing to her, exclaimed, "You're sad!" At this, Janice and I burst into giggles. "Good job!" I said.

Nora had her hands full with four tiny children. To make matters worse, she was disorganized by nature, and to make matters even worse, Artie was a neat freak. He absolutely could not stand the chaos. Moreover, Nora's personality was such that when she got flustered, whatever level of order existed degenerated. Artie's dissatisfaction had her almost falling apart. They were not talking. I saw them individually for quite some time. Finally, I met with them together. They were very polite and full of hope at this joint session. I asked them to each make one request of the other. Artie, of course, asked for some effort at creating order and even offered to help. The next week, Nora tried to tell him that it took quite a bit of organizing just to enable them to come to the session that evening. "Give him a list of what you did," I suggested. "Well, I got a babysitter, and I was able, over three separate attempts, to pump two ounces of milk for the baby." "Wow, with all those kids wanting attention!" I said. Then I asked Artie, "Can you even imagine what effort that must have taken?" With a straight face, Artie replied, "I pumped an ounce once."

Laughing is a great habit to acquire.

> **(Tool 127, again) How to Laugh #1**
> Just laugh.

Chapter Sixteen
Increase Your Sensitivity

Brain researchers at the University of Iowa had sixteen people playing cards with decks that they didn't know were rigged. They were hooked up to an electrical skin conductance monitor which started going crazy after the tenth round although the players weren't consciously aware of it. Their subconscious knew before they did. It took something like eighty rounds for ten of the sixteen people to "realize" that the deck was rigged.[1]

Sensitivity is the ability to *sense*, to take in information—and be aware of it [Refer to Chapter Six, My Partner Is Hypersensitive, p. 71]. Most of us are oblivious to how the people in our lives feel and what's on their minds. We don't even know what *we* feel. Like the people in the experiment, we may know at some gut-level, but we aren't aware of it.

And that's too bad. The greater our level of sensitivity to ourselves and to our partners, the better. Knowledge is power.

Sensitivity, however, comes with a price tag. If we are aware of what's below the surface, we're liable to feel painful feelings. On the other hand, when we allow ourselves to feel pain, then we can feel joy. So it's worth the price.

1. Sensitivity about Oneself

Let's take a look at Ricky's sensitivity. At the beginning of our story, Ricky knew very little about himself. He was not aware that he was distressed was because his wife's look triggered feelings of his mother's coldness. Had he realized this about himself, he could have dismissed the whole thing with, "Whew! I felt for a minute like a little kid again! But Jean is not my mother. Jean has never rejected me." (Tool 12)

Ricky's lack of awareness was a childhood coping mechanism which pushed out the unbearable thought, "My mother doesn't want me." When Jean gave him "the look," it triggered the unbearable feeling of being rejected, although he did not recall his childhood experience.

Had he remembered what caused the awful feeling, he would have acted differently.

How well tuned into your feelings are you?

(Tool 132) Checklist: Take This Test of Your Sensitivity Level to Yourself	
1. Do you know why you cry?	
2. List the movies you don't want to see and why.	
3. What does your partner do that upsets you. Why?	
4. What do you like sexually?	
5. When you're getting tired, what do you experience? What tells you?	
6. How can you tell when you're about to have overeaten but before you're stuffed?	
7. Why does your work make you happy/unhappy? List.	
8. What are your preferences regarding noise level, temperature level, going to bed late, or getting up early? List.	
9. How many activities can you juggle at once without getting confused or losing your cool?	
10. Can you sense danger? How do you do that?	

11. What do you like/dislike about your neighborhood?	
12. Who is your favorite person and why?	
13. What three things keep you where you are professionally?	
14. socially?	
15. Why is it that you have a lot of/few friends?	
16. Think of something someone says that always ticks you off or hurts your feelings. Why does that tick you off or hurt your feelings? Where did the problem come from? Would it bother other people?	
17. Do you meet your own standards? Why or why not? Where did those standards come from? Do you objectively agree with them? Are they correct for everyone or just you?	
18. How do you feel about your relationship with your children? Do they give you joy? What can you do if they don't?	
19. Did your father have different expectations from you than your mother? What were/are they?	
20. Does driving in traffic make you angry? Why or why not? Why would the stupidity of other people on the road be a reason to make you angry?	

You can see that "sensitivity" means "awareness." Awareness of the patterns of behavior that others usually exhibit and why. Awareness of the feelings that go with those patterns. That awareness doesn't come very easily. There are blocks to adequate sensitivity which must be overcome.

➢ Playing victim

When you play victim, you *substitute* a reason that you made up for the real explanation of the other person's behavior. That substitution prevents you from allowing all the information to get through to you. When Ricky was confronted with his wife's fatigue, he ignored it. He substituted something he made up, that she was rejecting him, for the simple reality.

When Cameron became angry at his wife, Sharon [Refer to p. 189], *because she could stay home with the children while he worked so hard, he was playing victim. What he didn't consciously connect was that when he was growing up, he had to shoulder a lot of responsibility while it seemed his younger sister got off easy. He always resented the unfairness of that. His wife being home triggered those old feelings. To handle this better, he needed more self-awareness.*

Another pitfall of playing victim: It blocks information.

(Tool 133) Reflect on This . . .
Now that you have heard me discuss victim thinking in depth, can you remember what your partner said was the real reason for things? Can you see how you substituted your victim thoughts for your partner's real reason? Make a list from the last thirty days.

➢ Fear of feelings

If you are afraid of pain, you will not be open to new information when it requires awareness of your feelings.

The solution, of course, is to take the plunge and feel feelings because, along with the bad ones, there will be good ones. Take your "emotional temperature" four or five times a day. Just stop what you are doing and ask yourself how you feel. Make a list of all the feelings you are experiencing. Connect what is going on at the moment to the feelings.

In addition to using Tool 106, Ralph [Refer to p. 163] has been working hard on allowing himself to feel all his feelings. It's been very trying. When he feels ugly and undesirable, as he does when Sandy won't have sex with him, it's hard to allow those feelings to persist. Yet, in order to get past them, he must recognize them. When he feels them now, he tells himself, "Sandy has a right to feel hurt because I did hurt her. She's not rejecting me; my actions pushed her away." This makes him feel sad and he allows himself to feel that sadness without letting it turn into depression. (To prevent depression he has to use his tools to stop victim thinking.) He reminds himself, "I'm working on treating her well. It has been a long time since I slipped. I'm getting there." Although the sadness isn't a good feeling, when Ralph feels sad, it's so much better than the explosion of anger that used to overtake him without warning. Yesterday, Sandy told him she really appreciated how he was trying. He noticed a little whoosh of delight stir inside him.

Feeling is exhilarating.

(Tool 134) Reflect on This . . .
Are you comfortable with your feelings, even bad ones? What are you feeling right now? Take your emotional temperature four or five times a day and keep a log of your feelings.

---

2. Sensitivity to Others

If you have learned, through the pain of experience, to push away your feelings, you will certainly not understand the feelings of others. Picking up cues from other people and *accurately* interpreting their meaning—or asking—is absolutely necessary.

There are blocks to developing sensitivity to others.

➢ Not looking

In a scary interpersonal world, it may be easier to watch television than look at your partner. But looking is the most important source of information we have!

What color outfit is your partner wearing? What expression is on your partner's face? Voice? Body?

Yes, this task could be aversive if you have gotten into disputes every time you made eye contact. But if you have both been going through this book, now is the time to experiment with looking at each other again.

Poor Joshua [Refer to pp. 105-106, 115, 119-120, 139, 141]. *In trying not to look at the mess that Arianne couldn't seem to straighten, Tool 67, he had stopped looking at Arianne. He eventually made her feel invisible. His contradictory body language (Tool 77) confused and upset Arianne. His mind was taken with Chu Hua, a single woman who had walked in his office door. For his marriage to get back on track, Joshua decided he had to look at his wife while managing to overlook the mess.*

Something unexpected happened. The more Arianne was aware of Joshua looking at her, the better she felt. She started to smile. Over time, her dark mood started to lift. Joshua noticed that—and he responded to it. He started to notice a spark inside when he looked at his wife that he hadn't felt in a long time.

He allowed the memory of Chu Hua to fade. The next time he saw her, he was amazed at how indifferent he felt.

Eyes are windows to the soul; start looking at them.

(Tool 135) Reflect on This . . .
Do you look at your partner? Start taking in information.

> ➢ Unwillingness to grow

If you believe that you can continue to learn and grow until the day you die, then you will. If you think you know it all, you will not "see" new information. When new information comes, you will automatically "file" it where the old, familiar information went. Then you'll be taken aback when something you should have "seen" hits you in the face with too much force.

That's what happened to Dylan Klebold's parents. They thought they knew how to raise kids and didn't need new information even though their child was withdrawn and unhappy, and spent an inordinate amount of time in his room. The old child-raising knowledge said to see a psychiatrist who will write a prescription, so they did that. Now, they've surely done everything.

Except they didn't. If you remember, Dylan Klebold was one of the Columbine killers. Klebold's parents are quoted in a book by James Garbarino, a psychologist at Cornell University, and co-author Clare Bedard as saying that they have nothing to apologize for because that isn't the way they brought up their child.[2]

Surely, they didn't *intend* to bring up their child to be a mass murderer, but in thinking that they did "everything," they shut the door on growing as parents. They needed to leave room for new questions and new possibilities: Maybe giving him meds wasn't enough. Maybe the child needed to talk to someone. Maybe the child needed supervision.

Growth can be scary. It means maybe you haven't done enough. Maybe you haven't done "everything."

Are you open to growing?

> **(Tool 136) Reflect on This . . .**
> How open are you to hearing something you wouldn't have expected or wanted to hear? How open are you to stretching yourself? In what areas do you think you need to grow? What have others told you about this?

Assuming that you have overcome all of the obstacles to being a sensitive partner, you should do very well on the following checklist.

Enjoy the warm tickle inside when you get these right:

(Tool 137) Checklist: Take This Test of Your Level of Sensitivity to Your Partner	
1. Are you right nine out of ten times when you read your partner's expression? Give examples of what different expressions mean.	
2. When your partner is unhappy, do you realize it before she tells you? What does she say usually?	
3. Do you know your partner's favorite food, color, beverage, movie, TV program, clergyperson, vacation spot, music, way of relaxing? List them.	
4. Do you know exactly what your partner likes to do first when coming in the door? What is that?	
5. Do you know which expressions to avoid? What are they?	
6. Do you know what she expects of you most of the time? What?	

7. Do you know how to turn her or him on? Yes/No	
8. What makes your partner happy? List.	
9. What makes your partner unhappy?	
10. How does your partner feel about your respective roles vis-à-vis your children? Or step-children?	
11. From your partner's perception, who bends more to make peace? Do you agree? If not, why does your partner see it that way?	
12. Do you both see the effect of your in-laws the same way? How about your parents?	
13. Look at your partner's biggest gripe; why does he hold it? Describe from your partner's viewpoint.	
14. Why did your partner decide to marry you (from his viewpoint)?	
15. Do you believe your partner loves you? Is your belief consistent with what he says? If not, why not?	
16. What are your partner's needs? List.	
17. What can you do differently that your partner never mentioned? Why do you think this would work?	
18. What are your partner's biggest dreams, career-wise?	
19. What are your partner's life dreams other than career?	
20. What is your partner's highest held ethical value?	

Being sensitive to oneself and being sensitive to others is a balancing act. If it's lopsided, there will be trouble. Too much awareness of one's own feelings can make a person lose sight of the other person's feelings. Too much awareness of one's partner's feelings (and needs) can result in losing oneself.

Balancing feeling your own pain and joy with that of your partner will result in a very healthy relationship. Do you remember Sonny and Vivian who lost a son (Tool 129)? In their grief, they only felt their own pain. This is normal and natural. But as they picked up the pieces of their lives, they included others and did so with more and more verve. In the end, their sensitivity to themselves was well-balanced with their sensitivity to others.

Part IV:

Rebuilding Your Marriage

Saving a marriage is about eliminating bad behavior, but it's more than that. It's about healing, but it's more than that, too. It's about creating something you never had before, something new and good. It's about discovering how a couple can be more than the sum of two individuals.

Chapter Seventeen
Sixteen Things to Do to Reconciliate
—and Ignite that Spark!

You have both worked hard. Most of the hurtful behavior is gone. Pain is dished out less frequently. There is backsliding; that's normal. But the direction is positive. And now you're entitled to ask, "Is that all there is? – No more pain? Well, I could get a novocaine for that." The answer is: No, your marriage should be happy, sparkly, close, and loving. That's the next step and that's what this chapter is about.

1. Reach out.

Do you feel like you are the only one in the relationship that's trying? It's a tough, lonely place to be, isn't it?

It shouldn't be like that. That is like someone rowing a boat on one side: It turns around and goes nowhere.

So, reach out and engage your partner in the process. The burdens become shared burdens; the benefits, mutually enjoyed. If you've gotten this far in the book without your partner's participation, now is the time to reach out.

True, you've learned many things. But there are three problems with reading it alone. One is that you may be thinking, "See, here's an example of something he should be reading!" Instead of reading it so as to learn and grow yourself, you might be finger-pointing. That's no good.

The second problem with reading it all alone is that your partner is missing out on a whole new world of happiness. And the third problem is that so are you.

If you have truly worked on yourself and anyone could see that, then now is the time to develop some strategies for engaging your partner. Here are some options.

- Come right out and say she should read this book.
- Tell your partner—with kindness and compassion—that he is obviously unhappy in the marriage and that the book has answers.
- Leave out a page or two on the table for your partner to read.
- Surprise your partner by approaching an old subject in a healthier way and then explain that you have learned something from the book.
- Ask pointed questions to get your partner to think, such as, "If you don't want to read this book, what do you want to do to save our marriage?"
- Get her curiosity aroused by making references to page numbers or topics covered in the book. Don't do this in a superior way, of course.
- Make references to the love you have or had for one another and the need to find that love again.

To handle this right, you must be well healed. Then, if you get a nasty response to your loving invitation to join you in this effort, remember that your partner has not been healed and has no understanding of what she is doing. So don't take the nastiness personally any more: It is your partner's problem. You are merely trying to help.

Ricky and Jean

Suppose, for argument's sake, that Jean did not call a marriage counselor. Instead, she read this book, but Ricky didn't. Let's imagine the following difficult conversation:

Jean: Ricky, you are clearly unhappy in this marriage. I suggest you read this book.

Ricky: Oh, and a book is going to solve all my problems?

Jean: Maybe.

Ricky: That's ridiculous.

Jean: I don't have a crystal ball. Just read it and see for yourself if you get anything out of it.

Ricky (imitating her tone of voice) "Read it and see for yourself if you get anything out of it." Miss smarty-pants knows everything.

Jean (ignoring the rudeness because it is a tactic to distract from the conversation): You're avoiding the subject. I'm leaving the book here on the table.

[three days later]

Jean: Did you start the book?

Ricky: As a matter of fact, no. It's pointless.

Jean: Okay, you think it is pointless. Maybe you are right. But we loved each other once. And even though you are making me come to believe you no longer love me, I'd still like to give you a chance to help me make this marriage work.

Ricky: Oh, so you don't love me now?

Jean: That is actually in the book. It's right in the first chapter.

Ricky is curious. And he does love Jean, so when Jean isn't around, he opens the book.

Reaching out is challenging and emancipating.

(Tool 138) Reflect on This . . .
How can you engage your partner in this marriage effort?

There are other times to reach out as well. Suppose you have had an argument. How do you make up? Who initiates that?

In our story, after Goldie arrived, Jean could have lovingly told Ricky that she is not rejecting him because she is not up for sex. She could have told him that when she says she is tired, it's true.

She also could have tried to be warm in spite of her fatigue. Maybe that would have given Ricky the message that she was not mad at him, just exhausted, as she said. Reassuring him she really *was* tired is hard because reaching out requires strength. Now she somehow has to muster up the energy to recognize her fatigue and approach him to soothe him. Where will she get that strength from? Why is it her responsibility to approach him? Why should she always be the healer?

The answer is it's not her responsibility, and she shouldn't have to be the one to make the first move all the time. But when a couple is down in the dumps, when a relationship is getting messed up, someone has to reach out. If the same person always reaches out, then after they have resolved the issue, that person could say, "You know, it's always me that initiates resolving our problems. That's not fair. Next time we fight, it's got to be your turn to start the conversation."

Go for the gold—and don't be surprised when you get it.

> **(Tool 139) Reflect on This . . .**
> Let your partner know that it is fairer for both of you to take turns initiating reaching out after an argument.

2. Do five nice things for your partner this week without counting how many were done back to you.

Counting is a temptation. By doing something nice and waiting for a response, you are trying to jump past the need-to-heal hurdle. The tit-for-tat should come—eventually—when the relationship is on a solid footing.

But right now, healing means giving and expecting nothing back.

Imagine a bank account that is in the negative. That negative number stands for "personal resources." Your partner's personal resources are beyond empty; they're owed. No matter how good a person you are, if your partner feels owed, you have to give first before you can get back. Even a "thank you" may be too much of a drain on your partner's negative balance.

Richard was a good man. He tried to do his best. But he thought it's only natural to get acknowledgement back. His wife, Cecile, a more reserved person, figured that if she worked hard and he worked hard then there was no reason to thank him. After all, if she spent the day taking care of the children, did he thank her? So even if he went out of his way for something, an extra item on the household list that required he search online for three hours, for example, she didn't acknowledge it. Her day started early and ended late; so did his. From her point of view, they were even. Besides, she came from a cold family where efforts were just not acknowledged.

After the first few times this happened and Richard was stunned, he started to sink into depression. He was confused, hurt, lonely, and heartbroken. Sometimes he hated himself for these feelings; they seemed so wimpy. So he yelled at Cecile. He felt she deserved to hear how upset he was, how frustrated, how unfairly treated.

All this mystified Cecile. Where was this coming from? Why did she deserve such horrible treatment? She distanced herself even more from her husband.

As the two of them started working on themselves and started recognizing areas that needed change, the relationship went from distant and hostile to cold and neutral. Their emotional accounts were still negative!

This is where the healing must go into full gear and there was nothing in

217

reserve. But there was. That source of energy was "hope." They'd come so far, it was obvious that they could go further. Richard, who came from a warmer, closer family than his wife did, knew things could be better. He decided to pile on the unconditional giving. He did it with a smile.

Three months after this started, he could see the ice begin to melt. "He really is trying," Cecile thought. She smiled back at him, tentatively. His eyebrows went up. More hope fueled his bank account and he kept up the kindness.

Don't do it grudgingly. There will be no healing in that. If Richard can allow hope to give him the boost he needs, he can give with a full heart. If, however, he feels a grudge, then he needs to realize that to get to the good marriage he wants, he has to promote his wife's healing.

How did Richard get to a place where he could freely give? It started when he got a call that his friend, Bert, had had an auto accident and was taken by ambulance to the hospital. Richard dropped everything, shaking, and got in his car. His breathing was shallow as he rushed to the ER. He found Bert in a room, already bandaged up, with wires leading from various machines to him. One machine let out periodic beep-beep-beeps that started to drive Richard crazy. "How are you, man?" Richard asked. Bert whispered through a haze of painkillers, "I guess they don't want me upstairs, yet."

It crossed Richard's mind that this would not be the right moment to bring up the golf iron that Bert had "borrowed" some time ago and never returned.

During the time he was there, it was a whole production helping Bert to sip some water. They had immobilized him fairly well. It was in the silence of just being there with Bert that it crossed Richard's mind that a human psyche can get all banged up like that, too. How would the owner of such a psyche behave? Could such a person really function? Could he give to others? These thoughts were swirling through his mind as he got home, still shaken. A damaged psyche can barely sip the "water" that is offered, Richard realized. The decision to be Cecile's healer came swiftly without effort.

Don't be the giver out of fear. The purpose of this exercise is to start building good will where none existed. You can do good for your partner out of kindness and a genuine desire to be the good person that you are.

Dina wanted things to go well well [Refer to Chapter Ten, Scaring into Submission, p. 125]. *After all, they had four children and a twenty-year marriage. You don't easily let go of something like that. Dina was prepared to do whatever it took to make the marriage work. She considered doing something nice for David but she was still afraid of him. He had never laid a hand on her, yet his voice made her quake. She kept thinking that if she was only nicer, he would calm down; he would be nicer, too. Her counselor gently suggested that she encourage David to start at the beginning of this book and work on himself before she starts trying to appease the hungry tiger with treats. A relationship cannot be built on fear.*

Also, if your partner has not been working through the book with you and and continues to hurt you, then this tool is premature. Since he remains unhealed, he could interpret your kindness as a sign of weakness.

When I say "nice things," I'm not talking about getting tickets to a game where the seats are going for $200 a pop, although that certainly is a possibility. I am talking about little things like:

➢ Bringing in the mail and leaving it on your partner's desk
➢ Picking up the towel on the floor instead of expecting your partner to do it
➢ Fixing coffee and the rest of breakfast for your partner
➢ Running an errand for your partner
➢ Giving your partner a backrub
➢ Helping your partner at a social-business function when you'd rather not go

➢ Sitting through the type of movie you can't stand but your partner loves
➢ Going to the restaurant of your partner's choice for a change even if you don't care for their food
➢ Taking the vacation your partner really wants even if you don't
➢ Taking time away from your priorities to help your partner

Gerald had a heck of a trek to get to work. His job had relocated out of state but he and his wife, Sherrie, had just bought a new house. So, what with the distance and the traffic, his commute took almost four hours a day. He loved his work, but he knew he needed to start looking for something else. The problem of course was, how? When he got home, he was greeted by toys all over, a second grader sprawled on the living room floor fussing over math problems, and two tots bouncing and giggling on the couch. His wife was upstairs in the bedroom nursing their new baby. "Okay, kids, supper," Gerald announced. He did not know how to cook from beans. He went to the fridge and took out some cheese and bread. He spread the cheese over the bread and put it in the toaster oven. "Here you go," he told the children minutes later. They came to the table and ate their melted cheese sandwiches. Gerald went upstairs to check on Sherrie. She smiled at him, nodded at the slurping infant and smiled some more. "Thanks," she said, then yawned.

Kindness has infinite healing properties.

(Tool 140) Reflect on This . . .
What kind deeds can you do for your partner? What does she want? Does it make you feel badly to do that after so much pain? Or can you enjoy the renewal of the relationship?

---

3. Understand that your partner's viewpoint is as valid to him as yours is to you.

People have the (incorrect) assumption that "the way I see the world is the way it is." No, everyone has his own perspective on the world and everyone thinks their own is the right one. That is okay. I can think my worldview is right as long as I'm aware that you think yours is right with the same degree of conviction.

Here we are, thinking our worldview is not merely the right one, but the only one—and instead, our significant other sees it completely differently. And not only that, but our partner doesn't give squat for our view. Whew.

Do you remember Tom, the truck driver, and Linda, his wife? [Refer to pp. 131 and 137].

Tom realized that having dinner on the table meant the world to him. Linda couldn't fathom this. She operated her own business and it was growing rapidly. Her hands were full enough with the business and two children without thinking of dinner. And why was it her job anyway to make dinner? She probably made more money than Tom did! Besides that, if and when she could squeeze out time for herself, what she enjoyed most was going to the gym. That feeling of not having her head filled with thoughts, plans and worries was such a lift! Why, oh why did Tom have to focus so much on food? Indeed, Linda was a slim woman for whom food just wasn't a major source of joy.

But, understand it or not, agree with it or not, the reality was that to Tom, dinner on the table was a sign of love. And Linda loved Tom. The agreement they reached—to work on preparing the meals together and freeze them—suited her fine. She didn't mind defrosting and heating them for him. She even picked up fresh flowers if she happened to need some groceries that day. Heck, she also put on a music CD to go with dinner.

Deb Schwarz Hirschhorn, Ph.D.

Stretching yourself to see how the world looks from other eyes is a major step in building trust.

(Tool 141) Reflect on This . . .

How does your partner see the world? How is it different from your view? Can you imagine getting in her shoes for a minute and see the validity of the other view? Will you make a commitment to honor the other view by your actions?

---

4. Take ten minutes every other day to listen to each other thoughtfully and patiently.

This step is an outgrowth of the previous one. When you can respect your partner's viewpoint as much as you respect your own, then you are ready to have a real conversation. This means being attentive when you listen. It does not mean waiting patiently for your partner to be done speaking so you can speak. What's the point of that? If you both do it, then no one is listening to anyone, and there goes the whole point of a conversation.

Difficult as it is, listening provides a doorway into another person's head and heart.

(Tool 142) Reflect on This . . .

Be a good listener when your partner is speaking. Be genuinely interested.

If you're thinking, "But all my husband wants to talk about is the stock market and I don't know a put from a call," or "All my wife wants to talk about is our kids' behavior, which, I agree is important, but is there no end to it?" or "All my partner wants to talk about is his mother and I'm out of ideas on dealing with her," then here are some ideas to consider:

➤ Learn about what your partner is interested in. Don't think of it as boring. Think of it as a way to expand yourself, much like traveling to another country. You don't have to live there, but you can sample the culture. By listening, you endear yourself to your partner, and who knows? You might even come up with responses that make the conversation that much more stimulating.

➤ The kids' behavior is deeply important. If you believe that your partner is doing something wrong in handling them, consult an expert together. And no, there is no end to talking about your kids—nor should there be. What's more, when you are a team and the contentiousness in the home is gone, you might find your kids' behavior to be a source of joy to discuss.

➤ If you do genuinely care about the topic at hand but you don't have answers, you might want to get another opinion on it. Alternatively, your partner may just need to vent and your willing ear will be good enough, even without answers.

Cherish what your partner says. Maybe then your words will also be cherished.

> **(Tool 143) Reflect on This . . .**
> Develop an interest in things your partner likes; by all means discuss your children; get help from experts if you are out of ideas; or just be a good listener.

Occasionally, you will have something urgent you want to express. At other times, you can let go and focus on your partner. That is highly flattering and will make her feel special in your eyes. This, in fact, is exactly how to treat someone who *is* special to you.

It usually took Ricky about a week of brooding to get over his bad mood. In the clarity that followed the last blow-up, he acknowledged to himself that his cocky attitude wasn't getting him anywhere. Besides, he did love Jean and he could see how his behavior was just making things worse for her, too. He decided to start reading this book. One idea in the book that he liked was being a good listener because then he wouldn't have to talk so much! The next day, he told Jean that he had started reading the book.

Jean: So what do you think so far?

Ricky: I like the idea about being a listener. What do you have to say?

Jean (surprised): There's a lot I could say. Where do you want me to begin?

Ricky: Anywhere.

Jean: When I say I'm tired, I'm tired. I wish you would believe me. I don't know why you don't.

Ricky (deciding that this conversation really should be about Jean): Why do you think I should?

Jean: Have I ever, in seven years, lied to you?

Ricky (thoughtfully): No, you haven't.

Jean: So that's my reason. Isn't that good enough?

Ricky has a lot to think about.

Being a listener not only enriches oneself but is a gift of the heart to the speaker.

(Tool 144) Reflect on This . . .
The fairness of taking turns does not have to occur in each conversation. Over the long haul, each partner should have an equal chance to talk, but in any one conversation, you may want to give your partner the complete floor.

If you are going to start having real conversations, stick to the ten-minute time frame. Don't try to do more or it might become too difficult to continue. It is easiest if you decide on a regular time or regular point in the day to do it. Make an appointment and put it on your calendar if you find you're not making time for it spontaneously. And let those ten minutes be real. Be in the moment: no phone, no kids, no computer, no interruptions.

Real conversations become a treat to look forward to.

> **(Tool 145) Reflect on This . . .**
> Come up with a good time for this ten minutes. People are more likely to stick to a new habit when they've made time for it. Put it in your calendar.

5. Be considerate and respectful. Your partner is not your slave.

It's crucial to express what you want and understand what your partner needs.

Express your needs politely and with the understanding that your partner's time and energy is as valuable to him as yours is to you.

Remember Cameron and Sharon from Chapter Fourteen, Eight Healing Activities for Your "Self"? [Refer to p. 190.] Cameron was a corporate executive while Sharon was a stay-at-home mother of four very young children. Cameron could, conceivably fall into the trap of thinking his time is more valuable than Sharon's because he works outside the home. In a loving home, how much money you earn is not the measure of value. Value is intrinsic to the person and therefore one person's time is as valuable as another's.

For that reason, no matter how anxious or stressed Cameron is, he needs to ask Sharon for help with the same good manners he would use in speaking to a colleague whose work he respects.

Cameron had another hard day at work, and it was going to be a long night. He brought work home with him. What he needed, in order to get a semblance of sleep tonight, would be dinner at his desk without the family. Of course, Sharon needed help with the kids and a break just to breathe and be her own person. Cameron made a point of slowing down when he walked in the door. He used to rush and that was upsetting to those at home; it conveyed anxiety. He took some deep breaths and attempted to get his body to relax. He smiled at the family.

"Look," he began, "I would appreciate a favor. I realize you've had the kids all day and you need a break, but Richards foisted this on me at the last minute and it's needed by tomorrow."

"Why didn't you tell him that's not reasonable?" Sharon wanted to know.

"See, this was DeLuca's project and he was working on it but his wife was in a car accident this morning and she's in the hospital. They threw it at me, and, frankly, I'm pleased. It's a sign that they respect my abilities to be able to take over this way. But I am afraid that since I'm not so familiar with it, it will take me longer than it would have taken DeLuca. So I'd like to just eat at my desk and work tonight. Will that be okay?" said Cameron.

Notice that Cameron has learned that his time is not more valuable than that of his wife and that requesting to not help with the children is a favor. Another point is that he ignores a potentially offensive comment that Sharon makes. When he asks for the favor, she assumes he failed to speak up for himself (*"Why didn't you tell him that's not reasonable?"*). He recognizes that he has thrown her a curve ball and she is a bit annoyed. Maybe the next day he can tell her that her comment wasn't nice, but this would not be the right time to do it.
In a marriage, respect is the coin of the realm.

(Tool 146) Reflect on This . . .
How will you phrase requests? How will you rephrase criticisms? What else will you do to show respect?

Another feature of the conversation between Cameron and Sharon, above, is the sensitivity we discussed in Chapter Sixteen. It means knowing your partner so well that you know what he needs. It also means filling those needs. You can't get out of this by saying, "Gee, I didn't think of that," because, by definition, that means you are admitting to being thoughtless. For the same reason, you can't say, "It's not something that I would have considered doing," because that makes you inconsiderate. In our scenario, Cameron was careful to come in the door slowly, not in the kind of rush that says, "It's all about me." He was careful, too, in how he phrased his request because he knew that Sharon would have wanted his company and his help.

How do you develop thoughtfulness and consideration?

If you have not been exposed to your parents being considerate of one another, or if your parents spoiled you growing up, then you have new ground to break. You must, at regular intervals during the day, as well as during specific events of the day, ask yourself: "Am I taking my partner's needs into account at this moment?"

The regular intervals could be once an hour or two, or they could be once in the morning, once in the afternoon, and so on. Events would include meal time, grocery shopping, and other specific moments when your partner's wants and needs should be taken into account.

Douglas liked to shop for bargains. He got a thrill out of grabbing a good deal, even if he didn't need the particular item at that moment. The grocery people all knew him. Because he was there so much, he learned to call his wife, Carol, to see if she wanted anything from the store. What's more, if it wasn't on sale, he still had to buy it for her.

Consideration means my partner is as important as myself.

```
(Tool 147) Reflect on This . . .
Consideration can be learned by checking in with your
partner at regular intervals or on recurring events, like
dinnertime, to ask what she wants or needs.
```

6. Do fun and meaningful things together regularly.

Marriage should be fun but it doesn't come automatically. Fun and joy need to be built into your marriage on a daily, weekly, monthly, and quarterly basis. Daily, there should be laughter; there should be space for jokes, talk, walks, exercise, games, or whatever you consider fun, together. My husband and I nearly always eat breakfast together and talk. It is peaceful then, before the day gets underway. Other people may enjoy sitting in silence at breakfast. Like the ten minute rule [Refer to p. 222, for #4 in this Chapter], don't allow interruptions during your together time.

On a weekly basis, there should be time for enjoying sex. If you have not gotten along for quite some time, that may be out of reach for a little while. However, as you see your partner trying and you, too, are trying, then enjoy this wonderful gift of marriage.

On a weekly basis, if you both find religious services meaningful, then that should not be skipped over in favor of chores to do. Spirituality can bring a couple closer together in many ways, from a walk on the beach to a trip to the science museum. Scheduling in things that you enjoy is as important as scheduling in things you have to do. Nourishing your souls together is a way to share.

Monthly and quarterly I am thinking of outings and trips. Time to get away from work, stress, and the ordinary events of your life is important. Movies, travel, sports, concerts, and volunteer activities can be enjoyed together.

Ricky and Jean

Ricky and Jean were doing better. They spoke with respect and good manners toward each other. Ricky started thinking more of how the world must look from Jean's viewpoint and Jean worked on understanding Ricky's past victim thinking. They were getting along and now they decided it was time for fun. They hired a well-recommended babysitter and went on a date. They just went to the movies, but it was so much fun to just get out. They decided to incorporate more of this good feeling into their day and organized their time to always eat dinner together. Sometimes Goldie sat in her baby seat next to them, taking it all in, but that was fine. They also decided to make time for each other, even if it was only ten minutes, at night after Goldie was in bed. If all they could muster was a hug, at least it was a hug from the heart.

You have to build in happiness.

(Tool 148) Reflect on This . . .
Come up with five to ten activities you would both like. Start making plans to put them into place.

---

7. Keep the positive things about your partner in mind to outweigh the negativity.

When you focus on the positive, you feel good; when you focus on the negative, you feel bad. That is not to say that a person should sweep the dirt under the carpet and pretend that things are fine when they clearly are not. But if you and your partner have been diligently working through this book then you are already seeing changes. Yes, it will take time for there to be less backsliding, fewer mistakes, more respect and consideration. Nevertheless, if you both are making an effort, then focus on that effort and on what has been accomplished rather than what remains undone.

You will feel better and have fewer fights when you focus on your partner's growth rather than her failures. Furthermore, focusing on the good—in

229

your own mind—causes you to interact with your partner in a pleasant, supportive way. This, in turn, brings out more of the behavior you had hoped to see in your partner.

If you are concerned that by not letting your partner know where she flopped you are condoning that undesirable behavior, don't worry because it doesn't work that way. Human nature is such that paying attention to unwanted behavior by complaining about it *increases* it, but ignoring it may decrease it. (Certainly, other factors come into play, but this is a good general rule.)

Now that Ricky was trying his best to be nice, Jean was worried about backsliding because last night he gruffly said to her, "You're never there for me!" First of all, it was just untrue. Second, it wasn't nice; it seemed as if he wanted to put a distance between them. Third, the fact that things had been going so well for them made her feel more vulnerable and hurt when he said that. She thought she ought to tell him that she was hurt and that his remark wasn't true. On the other hand, she wanted to follow the ideas in this book. She visualized Ricky's improvement, remembering particularly the recent conversation in which he asked her to speak her mind about anything she wanted. She remembered the fun they recently had, and that getting a babysitter and going to the movies was actually his idea. She smiled at the thought of it. Ricky noticed her smiling and smiled back. He reached out to hug her and she hugged him back.

Still smiling, she asked, "So when am I not there for you?"

"I'm sorry," Ricky immediately responded. "That was me in one of my moods. Just forget it."

Forgetting it wouldn't be easy after all they'd gone through, but focusing on the improvement in the marriage made it possible.

Thinking positively about your partner generates more positive.

> **(Tool 149) Reflect on This . . .**
> Name at least five major positive things about your partner.

8. Start practicing the fine art of solution-thinking.

Many people's thinking is problem-focused. It's "Oh, no, oh, no, this is terrible!" sort of thinking. This is negative and painful for those around you—and for you—and it goes nowhere. The thing that bothers you remains right there in full force, still bothering you.

On the other hand, solution-thinking means viewing problems as challenges. Sometimes there are no solutions. For example, when someone dies or is sick, you can't do anything. However, you most certainly can think differently about the situation.

The key to becoming a solution thinker is to force yourself not to dwell on how horrible the problem is. Simply leave space for solutions to appear. Sometimes taking a ten minute break from your work or your problem and doing nothing helps. Allowing your mind to wander creates room for solutions. This is a good moment to do the deep breathing and relaxation exercises. These, too, leave space for creative thinking and solutions.

Another approach is to ask yourself, "What needs to happen in order for the outcome I want?" Make a list of possibilities.

Do you remember Bernie and Melanie from Chapter One: Will the Real Victim Please Stand Up? [Refer to pp. 14-17.] Bernie was triggered by Melanie innocently asking him about his pay raise. Bernie immediately went to a dark place in his mind in which his father berated him. He managed to have a good conversation with her in which he asked her to phrase such questions differently in the future. When she explained to him that she only asked because she wanted to calculate tuition for their daughter's upcoming college education, he was relieved and realized that he had been reacting to a trigger that led to victim thinking.

Bernie realized that if he can get into the habit of finding solutions to problems, he will completely bypass the bad stuff.

Bernie's latest challenge is that the pay raise did not come through after all. This would be a perfect moment for him to fall into a blue funk. Sure enough, when the note came in his box that the raise was going to be delayed due to the economic situation and the precariousness of the company's position, he started to feel that familiar choking in his throat, a sign that the situation was a trigger. He even had the thought, "You've blown it again. Now what will you tell Melanie?" However, he realized that this was his abuser's voice, not his. He knew that he had been a good employee. The state of the economy was not his fault. He reminded himself of his accomplishments and took some deep breaths. He got a glass of water and felt better.

Logically, the next step would be to find a solution. He considered several:
1. Continue at the job while looking for a better one.
2. Continue at the job while starting an internet-based company.
3. Continue at the job while suggesting that Melanie take a part-time job herself since they were almost empty-nesters.
4. Do all of the above.

Bernie liked his list. And he liked even better the thought that he had come up with solutions instead of falling into his old, blue mood. Besides which, with solutions in hand, it could be the beginning of a productive brain-storming session with Melanie.

The more of a solution-person you are, the less stress your partner will feel, and the more grateful she will be to you.

Just as finding solutions requires hope, the presence of hope can generate solutions.

> **(Tool 150) Reflect on This . . .**
> What is positive in your present situation? List ten problems and either find a solution to each or find something positive about each.

9. Be cheerful.

Everyone is drawn to someone who is happy. Think of things that make you happy. Practice that every day. The more real your cheerful attitude becomes, the more of a magnet you become. Train yourself to look at the bright side of things.

Here's a picture I often draw for my clients: The Key to Happiness

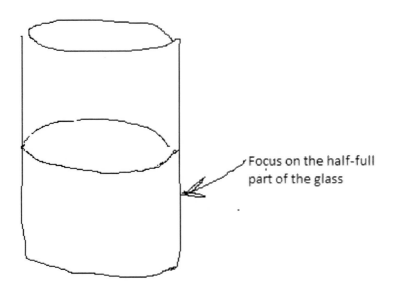

Focus on the half-full part of the glass

Copy this picture; it works! Keep it handy and remind yourself often of where your thoughts should be.

Good cheer is a blessing.

(Tool 151) Reflect on This . . .
In addition to the glass half full above, what three things can you do to get into a better mood?

At the beginning of our story, Jean needed a positive outlook as much as Ricky did. Even though things looked bleak, she needed to be happy with that darling little baby. She needed to force herself out of her blahs and focus on Goldie's sweetness and innocence and the possibility that that baby will have a better life than she and Ricky were having at that moment.

Keep a gratitude journal. Alternatively, every day when you wake up in the morning, be thankful for the goodness in your life and actually take time to list the good things you have.

Jean decided to keep a gratitude journal and look at it every day. Here is what she had on it: I am so grateful for-
1. my health
2. my energy
3. my adorable baby whom I love so much
4. the fact that Ricky is reading this book
5. what I have learned already from this book
6. that I can grow and learn more as life throws me curveballs
7. my job which is interesting and helps pay the bills
8. our home which is comfortable and has a mortgage we can afford
9. living in this country with all its freedom and opportunity
10. having delicious and healthy food to eat
11. that I do have Ricky in my life, whom I love

The goodness in your life is a gift. Always be cognizant of that.

> **(Tool 152) Reflect on This . . .**
> Do you count your blessings or look at the dark side of things? What can you do about it?

10. Trust

For Ricky to put his childhood past aside and accept when Jean says she's tired, he needed to trust her. For a person with childhood wounds, trust is almost impossible. He couldn't trust his own parents to take care of his hurt and help him through a difficult time in the life of his family, so why should his wife be trusted?

This is where a leap of faith comes in. He married her. He made a commitment to spend his life with her, for better or worse. She did the same. They were happy once. He has to believe in her honesty. He must work on trusting her.

To trust is similar to being positive: Often, you need to force your head into it. Like looking at the half-full side of a glass of water in order to become a positive thinker, you can make the decision to trust your partner in order to create a solid and loving marriage.

This is true even if your partner—or you—have cheated. If you are working together through this book and you are both committed to having a strong and happy marriage—and if you have seen some real changes—then you must take that leap of faith and decide to trust your partner.

If, after all this work together on the tools in this book, you are having a problem with taking this step, it is either because of your own history, or it is because your subconscious is telling you something you need to listen to. To straighten out which it is, you might need to get outside help. [Please see my website for additional resources: www.TheHealingIsMutual.com]

Once trust has been built, a marriage partner becomes a source of comfort and refuge from life's challenges.

> **(Tool 153) Reflect on This . . .**
> Do you trust your partner? In which areas do you have trust and in which areas don't you? What can you do to improve your sense of trust? What can he do? Make a list for discussion.

11. Pitch in to help.

It takes self-discipline to be helpful around the house. I don't know too many people who like housework. In spite of this, chores get done. (Usually, it's the wife who gets things done, and that's because she was trained as a little girl to do so.) All the strength, honesty, trust, and logic in the world will not solve this problem without the self-discipline necessary to be a responsible, equal partner in the housework.

The self-discipline begins with looking at the condition of the house and working off a mental checklist of what needs to be done. It also requires communication between spouses as to what an acceptable level of order or disorder is for each person. Then, of course, everyone has to actually roll up their sleeves and do the work.

Ricky's attitude about not helping may have been the result of patriarchy, a thinking process that says housework is woman's work. Nevertheless, the individual family plays a huge role as well. More than half a century ago, *my* father got up in the middle of the night to change my diapers and feed me because my mother was hard of hearing. Rather than wake her, he just did it himself, with love and compassion both for me and for my mother. I see social pressure as less of a force on us than our own families.

Ricky lacked the awareness that he needed to participate in housework because his mother was too busy licking *her* wounds after his father left to pay proper attention to him. When his father left, he left behind his responsibility to be a dad as well. Ricky didn't learn these skills because his parents didn't teach them to him, but now the responsibility to make up for that must shift to his own shoulders.

An excellent book on the teamwork in happy marriages is Peer Marriage by Pepper Schwartz[1], a researcher on what makes marriages work.

Empowerment can come from overcoming one's own laziness. Being able to do that is much like going to the gym and doing more than you ever thought you could.

(Tool 154) Reflect on This . . .

Do you have self-discipline? In which areas of your life do you have it? Does it extend to the chores necessary to run a house? Admit the truth! What can you do about it?

Helping, though, is a two-way street. A wife who is better at some things than her husband should not hesitate to help him in those areas. The decision to help is an indication of kindness and caring as much as it is an indication of overcoming laziness.

A marriage in which both people help and both people get the help is balanced and healthy.

(Tool 155) Reflect on This . . .

Do you chip in to help or are you used to being the one that gets the help? Can you stretch yourself to take on a new role?

---

12. Show affection

Let's talk about love. When two people meet and fall in love, what they feel, besides the fact that they have things in common to talk about is that this other person is interested in *them*. Falling in love massages egos. That's not bad – good marriages come out of it.

But love, real love, is something more. Falling in love is all about *me*, how this other person makes *me* feel; love is all about *the other person*. It's about giving. Obviously, when you give, if the marriage is functioning well, you get back. But it begins with your giving.

For example, think of the love parents have for their children. It is about giving without thinking about getting back. The same must be true of marriage in order to to move past no more pain to creating sparks. For love to bloom and passion to be ignited, it's got to start with giving without concern about what you get back.

Giving love can start with affection. Remember #1 in this chapter was "reach out"? Affection is a more personal way to reach out.

However, there needs to be something called "consent." Your marriage used to be troubled. Now it is in the process of healing. In order for the healing to go well, both of you must be on the same page. That is why you need to talk and spend time together having fun. If you or your partner is not ready for physical contact, then be patient and put into place the rest of the tools in this book. It could take six months to a year of a pain-free marriage before one of you is ready even for a hug. This is a very individual thing.

If, on the other hand, you are both ready for it, then here's how to start: with the level of warmth you would give any loved one. Judge your partner's comfort level [Refer to Chapter Sixteen, Increase Your Sensitivity, p. 201] before moving on to physical contact.

Do you remember this part of the dialogue between Jean and Ricky from #7, above?

Ricky noticed her smiling and smiled back. He reached out to hug her and she hugged him back.

Still smiling, she asked, "So when am I not there for you?"

"I'm sorry," Ricky immediately responded. "That was me in one of my moods. Just forget it."

Forgetting it wouldn't be easy after all they'd gone through, but focusing on the improvement in the marriage made it possible.

The path that this couple is taking is typical: a few steps forward, one step back. Learning is never on a smooth line. Because Jean was keeping "the good Ricky" in mind, she happened to smile at him in spite of his unpleasant, unfair, and untrue complaint the night before. He immediately reached out to her with a hug.

She could have said, "I'm not in the mood. You hurt me yesterday." Instead, she reciprocated the hug. Why did she? Because igniting the spark again means focusing on the good (#7) and giving freely of yourself, Jean put herself in the mood to reciprocate that hug.

The beauty here is that Jean's hug was honest. She was connecting in her mind with the good person that Ricky is when she gave it. And she benefited from taking that step because he immediately apologized for the previous night. Had she been angry with him for it, his defenses would have been up and the argument would not have ended.

Little gestures of warmth mean the world.

(Tool 156) Reflect on This . . .
Sparks of love and passion come from affection and positive thoughts about your partner.

---

13. Accept—and cherish—the differences

When you first met, it wasn't what you had in common that excited you, it was the differences. No one says, "Sameness attracts." No, it's "Opposites attract." So it's unfair if, after years of marriage, the very same things, the *exact* things that attracted you become a source of annoyance.

Now you're going to tell me that it isn't the same things, but different things that annoy you, things that you didn't even know about. And I will say that those things you didn't know about are really part of the whole picture of your partner.

For example, if Ricky appealed to Jean because of his strong, silent persona, then his going off to his room to sulk was totally consistent. If Jean appealed to Ricky because she was sure of herself and independent then her painting the living room without his okay after a few attempts at talking to him was also totally consistent.

Some more examples: If Sharon was attracted to Cameron (#5) because he was a very capable, responsible person, then she should not be surprised if he brings work home. If Tom was attracted to Linda (#3) because she was a very capable, responsible person, he shouldn't be surprised if she was busy making a living instead of fixing dinner. If Carol was impressed by how Douglas (also #5) grew up in poverty and made his mark on the world, then she should see his looking for bargains as part of the same picture.

One of the things that attracted me about my husband was his humor. I really needed a dose of humor in my life. So why should it bother me if he makes a joke about the things that I take seriously? Isn't that why he was hired for the job? Maybe I am the one who needs to lighten up!

Every time you get annoyed by the things your partner does, remind yourself that this was part of the package when you fell in love. If you dig deeply enough, you will see how the very qualities that annoy you now are connected to the original sources of attraction.

It was a gorgeous summer night. Aaron did not want to attend his aunt, Cleo's party. He did not want to be her pet project, her new immigrant nephew with the broken English, but he put his best foot forward, took a deep breath and walked through the garden to the back where the band was playing.

Cleo introduced him to some of her friends, a mixture of all ages, and then she left. People in Cleo's generation trailed off, leaving Aaron alone with the most beautiful girl he had ever seen. She introduced herself as Cassie. She was quiet and shy, but it turned out she had just graduated Harvard. That did spike his interest. How could one girl be so beautiful and smart too?

Cassie was fascinated with this brave boy who came across the ocean. Her own life was so structured! His freewheeling approach to life attracted her.

They started dating. Eventually, they married.

Fast forward fifteen years. Aaron is complaining to his best friend, "She always makes me feel so stupid. No matter what my accomplishments, she shoots down all my ideas. She has ten reasons why they are no good."

Meanwhile, Cassie complained to her friend, shaking her head, "I don't know where Aaron gets his ideas from. They are so out of left field."

Smart people don't necessarily dismiss other people's opinions. But when Aaron flipped over Cassie, he didn't concern himself about how she used her brains. He was just attracted to the fact that she was bright. Now, that doesn't seem so attractive. Aaron needs to remember that what swept him off his feet in the first place was Cassie's intelligence. Maybe he could help her channel her quick mind into a more constructive approach to examining his ideas. Between the two of them, perhaps they could really generate some good concepts.

For her part, Cassie needs to remember that the "left field" was part of the intense attraction she experienced when she first met Aaron and that renegade approach to life kept her interest for years into their marriage. Rather than shoot down his ideas, she needs to cherish his free-wheeling mind and see if the two of them could meet half-way.

Harness the sexual energy of "viva la difference!"

(Tool 157) Reflect on This . . .

Make a list of all the qualities in your partner that annoy you and trace every one of them back to what attracted you in the first place. Get help from those who know you both well and may be more objective if this proves difficult.

14. Find common interests, values, passions, and goals

Balance is a key to happiness. Now that you have worked hard on Tool 157—which is a work in progress that you should keep in mind for years to come—make space in your head for its exact opposite: commonality. Commonality is boring but stabilizing. Commonality is what keeps us from loneliness. The more we have in common with our partner—in spite of the excitement of those differences—the easier it is to understand one another and the easier it is to decide which house to buy or where to send the kids to school. The more in common, the less disputes, the smoother life goes.

If there were no differences, I assure you it would be excruciatingly boring. There has to be a balance, a fine demarcation point in the number of things that are different and the number that are the same.

Marriages work best where the couple has ethical and religious values in common. Issues of honesty, loyalty, degree of conservatism in religion and culture should be more or less on the same page.

It is nice if the couple shares goals such as where to live, how to retire, and what they each want to do with their lives. But it's also okay if they have differences in this area. Such things are negotiable and each person will be enriched by hearing the other person out.

Shana thought she had nothing at all in common with her husband, Daniel. He was a stock trader who, it seemed, could work up a sweat just looking at a ticker. Okay, she agreed he did very well at what he did, but they certainly couldn't talk about it. And then when weekends came, if he was nice enough to take her out, he'd want to go to those bang-bang kill-'em movies that made her insides churn. She couldn't bring herself to go unless she was willing to lose sleep for a week. Otherwise, he was happy going to play football with his buds and she was home alone with little kids. Vacations were the same problem. She'd rather sit on the beach and soak up the sun; he wanted to explore and see the surroundings.

Shana wondered how she could tolerate the loneliness any longer and confided in her friend, Sarah. "Gee," Sarah commented, "I didn't see it that way. You've got the children in a good school. Didn't you select that school together?"

"Oh, sure," Shana answered.

"I thought so," said Sarah. "And you go to religious services at a place you both wanted, right?"

"Actually, we both enjoy it there very much. We like the services and we've got friends there too. You're one of them," Shana answered.

"Right," Sarah said. "And how did you decide to take your mother in to live with you?"

"Well, we checked out nursing homes but mom wasn't ready for that. She

Deb Schwarz Hirschhorn, Ph.D.

can get around, and thank God she's all there. So it was Daniel's idea to have her come live with us," Shana replied.

"Really?" Sarah was surprised. "I didn't realize that. That's big. It doesn't bother him?"

"No," Shana said. "He said that my mother is our kids' grandmother and she's too important to be just left alone somewhere. I don't know. It doesn't bother him."

"Whoa," Sarah said, "I have to say, that's pretty impressive. Let me ask you another question. What's your plan for retirement?"

"I have no idea," Shana said. "That's something that never came up. I imagine Daniel will never retire," she chuckled. "He has so much energy."

"Right," Sarah responded, "he might do volunteer work or create a foundation, wouldn't he?"

"Yeah, I could see that," Shana said. "If he did, I'd be proud of him. I'd help him."

"So what's the problem?" Sarah asked.

"I guess the weekends are just bad, or half the weekends," Shana answered.

"So figure out something you enjoy, then. Why can't you do that? It seems to me you're making a mountain out of a mole's hill," she sniffed. Shana could see where her friend was coming from. Sarah's husband had a brain tumor; Sarah put all these trivia into perspective.

Shana decided that on beautiful Sunday mornings when her husband was playing football, she would go biking. She got a baby cart to trail behind and figured that would really be good exercise for her.

When she told Daniel, he was interested. "You, biking?" he asked.

"Well, I should get off my rear and get some healthy exercise, shouldn't I?" she came back.

"Absolutely. I think that's a great idea. I'd definitely go with you some of the time," he said.

"Well, great!" said Shana, pleased. She realized that Sarah was right: They had the important things in common and they could iron out the rest.

Wellbeing means getting clear on what's really important.

(Tool 158) Reflect on This . . .

Make a list of the "big" things that you have in common with your partner. You will be surprised at their number and importance. Next, make a list of the problem areas and search for alternatives that you might both enjoy in the realm of entertainment, free time, travel, and so forth.

---

15. Include one another in your daily doings

How much information do you keep to yourself and how much do you share with your partner?

It makes sense to hold your cards close to your chest if your partner has, in the past, used your sensitive information against you in times of conflict. However, you are now in Part IV of this book. Hopefully, that means you have both been working hard on making the dishing of pain a thing of the past. If so, one of the most important elements of intimacy and passion is friendship. You can tell a friend anything and that should be the case with your partner.

If that's not happening, there are three possible reasons: One, your partner is still hurting you. If so, you should not put yourself at risk. Continue working hard together on Parts I and II; do Part III alone, and then come back to this chapter.

A second possible reason you don't feel open with your partner is that although he is not hurting you anymore, it is a conditioned response for you to hold back. This is a normal reaction, a protective device. Time is the great healer in this one. Test the waters by sharing smaller things and see how it goes. Then test a little more.

A third possible reason for not sharing is that, like Ricky, you're just not used to it. You've fended for yourself a good deal of your life and the idea of expressing concerns, or even good feelings is strange to you. In spite of this, you can get used to sharing ordinary things. You can talk about your work situation and the personalities and politics there. You can talk about weekend plans. It doesn't have to be deep or emotional to qualify as including your partner.

For example, if a friend wants to visit, it's polite and considerate to tell your partner and see if that visit will be okay. If there is an event in the neighborhood that you want to go to, even if it is only for your gender, it is nice to mention that you want to go and find out if your partner will feel left out.

Here are some other ways to include your partner:
➤ Ask for his opinion on the news, aunt Laura's new house, or your kids' latest story.
➤ Ask your partner for help in doing a task.
➤ Offer your partner help in doing a task.
➤ Send your kids to their other parent for approval on something even though you would be capable of making that decision alone.
➤ Tell your partner the latest family or community information, appointments, and upcoming events.
➤ Invite your partner to functions that you want or have to go to.
➤ Share thoughts you have about your projects, plans, and concerns.

➢ Offer a willing ear so your partner can talk about her projects, plans, and concerns.
➢ Discuss birthdays, anniversaries and holidays together.
➢ Give a phone call during the daytime just to say, "Hi" if that is possible.

Francie came home, closing the door cautiously. In the "old days," before he was really working on himself, Kevin used to grump at her instead of saying, "Hello." Francie was anxious to tell her best friend her news. She had such a sense of urgency. And, at one time Kevin was her best friend. Then things had gone all sour for years. But now...was it really changing? She heard his footsteps approaching where she stood at the front door.

"Hi," she said, nervously. Kevin smiled warmly at her. Maybe he is my friend again, she thought.

"What's doing?" He asked.

"Kevin," Francie said, "I saw the doctor today."

"Oh? You didn't mention an appointment," he replied.

"I didn't want to worry you," Francie said.

"Well, how did it go?" Kevin's voice had a note of concern.

Francie took a deep breath. "They are concerned. They want to schedule more tests," she answered.

"OOO," Kevin replied. "I bet you're concerned."

That was all Francie needed. She had her old friend back. She broke down into sobs. "Yes, I am." Kevin put his arm around her. That was all he could do and all he needed to do.

Start thinking like your partner really is your other half.

(Tool 159) Reflect on This . . .
Include your other half in events, opinions, tasks, and plans.
Say, "Hi" just to connect.

---

16. Be patient

Improving your patience with your partner, yourself, and this process requires two things: learning to cope with stress and having a realistic time frame for positive changes—for both people.

In addition to the de-stressing techniques (Tools 29-35, 66, 77, 82, 85, 89-92, 119-122, 125-127, 131-136) discussed earlier, the one that may be most pertinent at this point is 131, to really be clear on the progress you have both made. Create a chart. Have you been nicer in your language? Has your tone improved? Be proud of the steps forward and don't get impatient over what is not going so fast.

When people come into my office and they fill out my intake forms, they discover that it may take six months, twelve months or even two years for the changes we are discussing to take place. Think of it this way: If you were a klutz, how long would it take you to become decent at tennis? Certainly two years of regular practice is not unreasonable. This book is all about learning new skills, seeing the world differently, feeling better inside and becoming graceful at doing all of this at once. It will take time.

Another way of looking at it is that putting all this learning into action is kind of like losing weight: They tell you not to weigh yourself every day or you will not see enough change to feel pleased. Put a note on your calendar every six months for the next two years to see how far you and your partner have come.

We can't force flowers to bloom.

> **(Tool 160) Reflect on This . . .**
> Recognize that learning—and putting what you learned into practice—takes time. Be realistic and evaluate progress based on what has been learned, not what hasn't.

Another consideration in overcoming your impatience is that if you are the partner of someone who has been very hurtful in your marriage, you, too, have been working on tools in this book. You have nurtured yourself and tried to be assertive. You have learned not to give it back the way your partner gave it to you because that would just duplicate the problem. You should continue to focus on your own progress. That will bolster your patience with your partner when you think his progress has slowed down.

Anne was getting frustrated with Jake. Why would he be so thoughtless after all this time? He'd been working through this book, learning so many techniques, but he still had guests drop in without consulting her. And he knew she was busy writing a grant proposal that needed to be submitted in two days. What in the world would she do with guests? She was steaming. And the guests would be arriving any minute. "How could you?" She shrieked.

Jake was startled. He'd been so occupied thinking about a big problem at work that he was trying to resolve, that he had no idea what Anne was talking about. Her tone sent chills up his spine. He looked at her in perplexity. "What do you mean?" he asked, catching his breath.

Now, Anne's blood was boiling. Hadn't he been working on being more considerate? Wasn't that among the reasons we got this book? How could he be so clueless? She remembered to take a deep breath. "You invited guests without consulting me!" She exclaimed.

"Not exactly," Jake explained. "I needed to talk to Reuben about this

project and he offered to come over."

"But you know I can't afford the time to play hostess to him," Anne said, her voice full of tension.

"I don't need you to. Don't worry," Jake replied.

"But I have to! What am I supposed to do, go in my room and look like I'm rude? You've put me where I have no choice but to be out there talking to Reuben and his wife. Yes, and why is his wife coming if it's business?"

"Oh, because they needed to go somewhere, I don't remember, and she would be with him."

"You see the position that puts me in!" Anne said more loudly.

"Okay, okay, I hear you," Jake replied, his volume rising. "Please stop yelling at me. Do your deep breathing; calm down. You're not being nice to me."

"I'm not being nice to YOU?" Anne was shouting now. "Oh, that's a good one. You're inconsiderate and I end up being the bad one."

Before they started working on themselves, Jake was abusive. There are no other words for it. And he got really far in making changes. He stopped shouting; he stopped name-calling; he learned to calm down; he stopped being judgmental of his wife—and himself. He improved greatly, but was he done? No. He needed to concentrate on the consideration, but it takes time. On this particular day, Anne was uptight and she let her husband have it. There's no way to justify her behavior. The saddest thing is that she didn't see her own errors. She was so used to thinking of her husband as abusive that it didn't occur to her that her tone all by itself was wrong. She needed to work on herself, too.

"Anne, you're right," Jake said. "I didn't think of where that puts you.

But I have to tell you the way you let me have it just now really shook me up. Wow, if that's what I used to sound like, no wonder I needed help. It's awful."

Anne did take some more deep breaths. Jake was right. She, too, needed to work on herself. After all, who is perfect?

It's amazing how an honest look at yourself improves your patience with your partner.

(Tool 161) Reflect on This . . .
To improve your patience, chart the progress you have both made, but then focus on your own growth rather than looking at your partner under a microscope.

Chapter Eighteen
The *Real* Law of Attraction

In Chapter 17 I started poking the surface of the concept of opposites attracting (#13 Accept—and cherish—the differences). I said that what annoys you now attracted you once. But the reality of why we are attracted goes way deeper than that. Maybe you are soul mates.

The concept of soul mates originated in the Biblical account of creation of the first people. According to the Biblical story, God indicated to Adam that in as much as it wouldn't be good for him to be lonely, he could use a "help, as if an opposite to him." Many Bibles mistranslate this entire phrase as "soul mate." The original is quite intriguing: These two people would be able to help one another by being opposites. In that way, one person's strength would bolster the other person's weakness. Together, they would get the job done that they were put here to do. They would be the perfect team.

Dare to think the possible: that you and your partner are soul mates.

(Tool 162) Reflect on This . . .

Can you remember your original attraction? What "opposite" qualities attracted you to your partner? List them.

In what ways would your opposite qualities make you and your partner the perfect team?

But, human beings being what they are, it isn't surprising that this efficient system broke down. No sooner did they get created, then they decided to do it *their* way instead of the way that God wanted. Not only that, they started pointing fingers at one another. In fact, the translation of Eve's role—even before she was created—could also be "help as if against him."

This doesn't surprise you, right? After all, here you are reading this book.

253

You know all about the "against" part. But why would Adam and Eve turn against each other? And what insight can we gain from the Adam and Eve story?

Adults who were hurt as children find examining their weak areas is particularly painful because it brings back all the old stuff—the criticism, blame, neglect, and other maltreatment. Therefore, they get insulted at the suggestion that maybe they need help in some area, maybe they don't know something. This would explain the guys who won't ask for directions. Or the women who insist they know how to get their kids to listen and won't get help from anyone else. Or the person whose marriage is falling apart and will not assume any responsibility for it. Failings, errors in thinking, not knowing something, trigger those old feelings of having deep personal flaws. This book has labeled this phenomenon "victim thinking." When victim thinkers are shown their weak areas, then the beautiful partner that they are supposed to love appears to them as the enemy, the one who is "against" them. Adam did the same thing. God gave him Paradise; the serpent tricked Eve; they both lost Paradise—and what did Adam do? He pointed an accusing finger at Eve. "It's all her fault," he complained. She, not his own poor choice, became "the enemy." Adam paid dearly for his mistake; we don't have to.

Dare to take help.

(Tool 163) Reflect on This . . .
How much of your relationship problems come from your inability to accept your significant other's helpful input?

But here is where the Biblical story holds out enormous hope. Recall that Eve was created to be a "help as if against him." Two small words that make a difference: *"As if."* She was never actually against him! When you can't seem to resolve issues it may really feel that way. But in *actuality*, your partner is not against you at all. It's an illusion which originates in your own perception.

Ricky and Jean

Let's see how this plays out with Jean and Ricky. In some ways he's tough and she's soft. In other ways, he's soft and she's tough. She deals with stress by burning it off in activities; he deals with it by moping and getting down. Both are escapes, but hers is healthier. He takes in stress to the boiling point, and he then erupts; she takes it in, and then she cries. She's also a connector to other people, more open than he is. (Note the close relationship with her sister and the immediate trust in the therapist.)

So she's attracted to his apparent strength, and he to her success at relating to others. When they met, he was fascinated by the magical way she opened him up, given that he was, admittedly, a taciturn person. She, in turn, took his quietness as a sign of inner strength (although she read that one wrong). She knew she is sensitive and wanted someone strong. He knew he is introverted and wanted someone who could pull him out of himself.

Although Jean and Ricky fit the paradigm of being opposites and attracting, they were bruised before they ever met; therefore, they saw one another as "against" instead of as helpers. It would be powerful if they saw each other as helpers instead.

Jean had a quality that Ricky could learn from: taking action when you're down. Jean took the initiative to paint when she was blue. Ricky would sulk.

Ricky had a quality that Jean could learn from: feeling love constantly no matter how bad things get. Jean was emotionally disconnected.

They each were in an incredible position to help the other and this help comes just by being who they are so that the other could imitate.

Do you remember the section on affection in Chapter 17? There, Ricky reaches out to hug Jean. She responds. At this point Jean has gotten past believing that Ricky is "against" her. She is following his example of constant love by reaching back out to him. She has already learned from him!

And in that conversation Jean teaches Ricky something crucial: to speak your mind. Ricky invites her to talk and she certainly does. Perhaps later on, Ricky might utilize this modeling of speaking your mind to tell Jean that he feels neglected. Let's make up a new scenario.

Things might sometimes backslide. That happens. If you can see it coming, that's when it's so important to pull out every good tool you've mastered. That's what Ricky did. Jean was working her usual job but because she was in retail, and the holidays were upon them, Jean was putting in extra hours. Ricky was a great dad. He picked up the slack with Goldie and even started preparing simple meals. Jean would shower and flop into bed, almost wordlessly. It was that coolness that bothered Ricky. He recognized his trigger and did not allow himself to fall into victim thinking. He waited until the holiday madness was over. When nothing had changed, he decided to speak to his wife. He took a deep breath as Jean was lying in bed, almost ready to drift off, and asked her if she could stay awake for just one more minute so he could talk to her. She agreed.

<u>Ricky</u>: Honey, I see how hard you are working and how tired you are. That's why I'm trying to help out.

<u>Jean</u>: You are and I appreciate it.

<u>Ricky</u>: But this feels like a repetition of when Goldie was born. You have nothing left over for me. I waited patiently through the holiday rush, and now what is the obstacle?

<u>Jean</u> (very thoughtfully): Nothing. Absolutely nothing. I just sank into old habits. Work, work, work. I didn't have to be so one-tracked. See, that's what you can teach me. Thank you, Ricky.

Ricky has learned that Jean is not against him. It seemed "as if" she was cold once again. Ricky realized that her body language (being tired, little conversation) almost triggered his old, destructive thinking (that she did not care for him). Luckily he recognized it for what it was. It was only "as if" she were against him. He was brave enough to open up a conversation on this very topic, and when he pointed out how she was slipping into old behavior, she thanked him. His ability to see beyond his triggers helped both of them.

Dare to admit your mistakes.

```
+------------------------------------------------------------+
|                  (Tool 164) Reflect on This . . .          |
|   Is it possible for you to see that your partner is not really |
|   against you?                                             |
+------------------------------------------------------------+
```

Healing

Marriage has healing properties. Even an awful marriage has within it the capacity to heal the bruises that were there *before* the marriage. This is healing of major proportions: Marriage can heal the bruises caused by the abuse in the marriage and the bruises that preceded the marriage.

The trick is to *see one another's oppositeness as a source of help.* Use all the tools you've learned in the seventeen preceding chapters and then add one more: Don't merely tolerate your partner's differences. Rather, recognize that you were not merely attracted to them; you needed to learn something important from them.

Suppose Ricky "gets it" and becomes a real team player as he seems to be doing, thinking of what to put on the grocery list, putting up the wash before the hamper overflows, and making dinners half the time. Then, over time, Jean will literally be healed. She will no longer suffer that feeling that she had since age sixteen of going it alone. His being by her side, sharing the responsibilities, will heal her.

Meanwhile, if Jean always consults Ricky, asks his opinion, shares her feelings, includes him in her plans, and makes him feel like a part of her, then, over time, he, too, will be healed. He will come to know in his bones that he will not end up alone, that he will always be part of Jean. He will believe women are okay people and he may even come to see his mother's behavior in a new and more compassionate light.

This is the secret of the way marriage is supposed to work.

Dare to give of yourself.

(Tool 165) Reflect on This . . .
What qualities do you have that could help your partner overcome early childhood pain?

Commonality

I've seen some couples for as long as a year, only to discover in separate visits with each one that they each had the same terrible secret—and neither knew.

There are all kinds of shared experiences that couples find out about each other long after the vows have been said: How both people lost a parent, or had a sibling that was killed, or were orphaned at an early age. One wonders how and why that happens. The answer is that there is a fundamental attraction to someone who knows on a deep personal level what your suffering is all about. It's as if your soul knew that no one else would understand you or relate to you but someone who's "been there."

I see this again and again with people and when I look at my own marriage, there it is. My husband's mother and my mother were very much alike in certain important ways. And although my husband and I are wildly different in personalities, we were given the same messages by our moms. Our moms tended to be critical while both of us had fathers that were highly supportive. Finding this out after years of marriage is breathtaking.

But it makes sense. If marriage is the place for healing, then who better to heal us than an opposite who is somehow very much alike in fundamental ways?

Beyond healing

When there is no more healing to be done, there still is growth. Life is growth. And sometimes growth is painful because it's hard to face your inadequacies. That's okay. We're all in that boat together.

You can actually enjoy your growth. Growth itself can be liberating instead of frightening. Uncovering your weak points can take on an "oh, well" perspective.

When couples come to enjoy this oppositeness and learn from one another, you notice that in long-term, happy marriages, they start to seem more alike. He starts to come out of his shell and she learns how to appreciate the quiet of her own mind. He talks more; she, less. She is a help to him, and he, to her. The opposite qualities of each help the other. And over time, their oppositeness is less real because they help each other meet somewhere in the middle. Eventually the oppositeness is only "as if."

You've started healing already and didn't see it.

(Tool 166) Reflect on This . . .

In what way(s) have you changed for the better due to the influence of your partner? In what way(s) has your partner changed for the better due to your influence? Where can you go from here? How can you help your partner to grow?

We were given a job to do here on Earth. Initially, we were supposed to tend the garden. After we left, our task was to create our own personal garden in our families. We made one mistake; we don't have to make more, but even if we have made a hundred mistakes, or a thousand, it doesn't matter. We still have another chance to get it right.

We can heal.

Together.

****

Please note that there are additional resources on my website: www.TheHealingIsMutual.com

----
Be sure to download the additional tools that I have mentioned earlier at www.TheHealingIsMutual.com/download.

INTRODUCTION NOTES

1 David R. Cook, and Anne Franz-Cook. "A Systemic Approach to Wife Battering," *Journal of Marital and Family Therapy* 10 (1984): 83-94.

2 Janet A. Geller. "Conjoint Therapy for the Treatment of Partner Abuse: Indications and Contraindications," in *Battered Women and Their Families: Intervention Strategies and Treatment Programs,* ed. Albert R. Roberts (New York: Springer, 1998), 76-96.

3 Chloe Madanes. *The Violence of Men: New Techniques for Working with Abusive Families: A Therapy of Social Action* (San Fransciso: Jossey-Bass, 1995).

4 Alan Jenkins. *Invitations to Responsibility: The Therapeutic Engagement of Men who are Violent and Abusive* (Adelaide, South Australia: Dulwich Centre, 1990).

5 Daniel Jay Sonkin, Del Martin, and Lenore E. Auerbach Walker. *The Male Batterer* (New York: Springer, 1985).

6 Michele Harway and Marsali Hansen. "Therapist Perceptions of Family Violence," in *Battering and Family Therapy: A Feminist Perspective,* ed. Marsali Hansen and Michele Harway (Newbury Park, CA: Sage., 1993), 42-53.

7 Etiony Aldarondo and Murray Straus. "Screening for Physical Violence in Couple Therapy: Methodological, Practical, and Ethical Considerations," *Family Process 33* (1994): 425-439.

8 Rebecca L. Schacht, Sona Dimidjian, William H. George, and Sara B. Berns. "Domestic Violence Assessment Procedures among Couple Therapists," *Journal of Marital and Family Therapy* 35 (2009): 47-59.

9 Lenore Walker. "Legal Self-Defense for Battered Women, in *Battering*

and Family Therapy: A Feminist Perspective, ed. Marsali Hansen and Michele Harway (Newbury Park, CA: Sage, 1993), 151-165.

10 Barbara J. Hart. "The Legal Road to Freedom," in *Battering and Family Therapy: A Feminist Perspective*, ed. Marsali Hansen and Michele Harway (Newbury Park, CA: Sage, 1993), 13-28.

11 Maureen McHugh. "Studying Battered Women and Batterers: Feminist Perspectives on Methodology," in *Battering and Family Therapy: A Feminist Perspective*, ed. Marsali Hansen and Michele Harway (Newbury Park, CA: Sage, 1993), 54-68.

12 Sue Lees. "Marital Rape and Marital Murder," in *Home Truths about Domestic Violence: Feminist Influences on Policy and Practice: A Reader*, eds. Jalna Hanmer et al. (New York, NY: Routledge 2000), 57-73.

CHAPTER THREE NOTES

1 Murray Straus, Richard Gelles, and Suzanne K. Steinmetz. *Behind Closed Doors: Violence in the American Family* (Garden City, NY: Anchor, 1980).

2 Murray Straus in email to the author February 15, 2007.

3 Aaron Larson. "Assault and Battery," *Expert Law* (October, 2003), http://www.expertlaw.com/library/personal_injury/assault_battery. html#2 (accessed August 22, 2010).

4 Caroline Johnston Polisi. "Spousal Rape Laws Continue to Evolve," *We News* (July 1, 2009), http://www.womensenews.org/story/ rape/090701/spousal-rape-laws-continue-evolve (accessed August 22, 2010).

5 Sheri Stritof and Bob Stritof. "Is Marital Rape a Crime?" *About,* http://marriage.about.com/cs/maritalrape/f/maritalrape10.htm (accessed August 22, 2010).

6 Murray A. Straus. "Leveling, Civility, and Violence in the Family," *Journal of Marriage and the Family* 36 (1974): 13-29.

7 Straus, et al., 1980.

8 Christopher M. Murphy, and K. Daniel O'Leary. "Psychological Aggression Predicts Physical Aggression in Early Marriage," *Journal of Consulting and Clinical Psychology* 57 (1989): 579-582.

9 The United States Department of Justice National Survey of Domestic Violence, published in 2000.

10 Straus, et al., 1980, vii-viii.

11 Irina V. Sokolova. "Depression in Children: What Causes It and How We Can Help," *Medical College of Wisconsin Health News* (December, 2003), http://www.personalityresearch.org/papers/sokolova.html, (accessed April 17, 2005).

CHAPTER SIX NOTES

1 Marlene Steinberg and Maxine Schnall. *The Stranger in the Mirror: Dissociation—the Hidden Epidemic.* (New York: Harper-Collins, 2001).

2 Howard J Osofsky and Joy D. Osofsky. "Violent and Aggressive Behaviors in Youth: A Mental Health and Prevention Perspective." *Psychiatry* 64 (Winter 2001): 285-295.

CHAPTER SEVEN NOTES

1 Ilyse L. Spertus, et al. "Childhood Emotional Abuse and Neglect as Predictors of Psychological and Physical Symptoms in Women Presenting to a Primary Care Practice," *Child Abuse and Neglect* 27 (2003): 1247-1258.

CHAPTER EIGHT NOTES

1 Bonnie E. Carlson, and Louise-Ann McNutt. "Intimate Partner Violence: Intervention in Primary Health Care Settings," in *Battered Women and their Families* ed. Albert R. Roberts (New York: Springer, 1998), 230-270.

CHAPTER NINE NOTES

1 Hart, 18.

2 Richard J. Gelles, and Murray A. Straus. *Intimate Violence* (New York: Simon & Schuster, 1988), 67.

3 Catherine Kirkwood. *Leaving Abusive Partners* (London: Sage, 1993), 44.

4 Elaine Leeder. *Treating Abuse in Families: A Feminist and Community Approach* (New York: Springer, 1994), 113.

5 Lenore E. Walker. *The Battered Woman Syndrome* (New York: Springer, 1984), 26.

6 Daniel J. Siegel. *The Developing Mind: How Relationships and the Brain Interact to Shape Who We Are* (New York: Guilford, 1999), 16-18.

CHAPTER TEN NOTES

1 John M. Gottman, et al. "The Relationship Between Heart Rate Activity, Emotionally Aggressive Behavior and General Violence in Batterers," *Journal of Family Psychology* 9 (1995): 227.

2 Straus, et al., 1980.

3 Mary Anne Banich Massey. "The Neuroscience of Fear," *Family Therapy Magazine* 8 (2009): 22-25.

4 Barbara J. Hart. "The Legal Road to Freedom," in *Battering and Family Therapy: A Feminist Perspective* ed. Marsali Hansen & Michele Harway (Newbury Park, CA: Sage, 1993), 13-28.

5 Bonnie E. Carlson and Louise-Ann McNutt. "Intimate Partner Violence: Intervention in Primary Health Care Settings," in *Battered Women and their Families* ed. Albert R. Roberts (New York: Springer, 1998), 230-270.

6 Murray Straus and Robert Gelles. *Physical Violence in American Families: Risk Factors and Adaptations to Violence in 8,145 families* (New Brunswick: Transaction Publishers, 1990), 426.

7 Bill Howatt. "Discussing the Stress Epidemic in Corporate America," in *Howatt H R Consulting* (2002). http://www.howatthr.com/images/ pdf/enhancingdna/Discussing%20the%20Stress%20Epidemic%20in%20 Corporate%20America.pdf (accessed March 9, 2011)

8 Joan A. Samuels-Dennis, Marilyn Ford-Gilboe, and Susan Ray. "Single Mother's Adverse and Traumatic Experiences and Post-Traumatic Stress Symptoms," *Journal of Family Violence 26* (2011): 9-20.

9 Karin AnneSchlee. "Wife Abuse: Disentangling the Effects of

Psychological and Physical Aggression," *Dissertation Abstracts International: Section B: The Sciences and Engineering* 61 (2000): 549.

10 Audrey R. Tyrka, et al. "Childhood Maltreatment and Telomere Shortening: Preliminary Support for an Effect of Early Stress on Cellular Aging," *Biological Psychiatry* 67 (2010): 531-534.

11 Jonathan C. Erwin. "Giving Students What They Need," in *Educational Leadership* 61 (2003): 19-23. http://posterous.com/getfile/ files.posterous.com/leadingedge/ik5zzohsERHdA5R6rqy2mmI3GZ GcM9v9A3F4C8bFj8o5mtrPEfAnI3DxkFnC/GivngStudntsWhtTheyNd. doc. (accessed March 9, 2011)

12 Roy C. Ziegelstein. "Acute Emotional Stress and Cardiac Arrhythmias," *Journal of the American Medical Association* 298 (2007): 324-329.

13 2005 WL 3508320, *T.T. v. L. DE J.* CN99-06525, Del. Fam. Ct.

14 Murray A. Straus. "Leveling, Civility, and Violence in the Family," *Journal of Marriage and the Family 36* (1974): 13-29.

CHAPTER TWELVE NOTES

1 Tim Roche. "Nate Brazill, Sentenced to Grow Up in Prison," *Time* (July 27, 2001). http://www.time.com/time/nation/ article/0,8599,169246,00.html (accessed May 26, 2011)

2 Meg Laughlin. "I Try to Be a Good Person," The Miami Herald, (February 8, 2004): 1A

3 Laughlin

4 Roche

Notes

CHAPTER FOURTEEN NOTES

1 Daniel J. Siegel. *The Developing Mind: How Relationships and the Brain Interact to Shape Who We Are.* (New York: Guilford Press, 1999).

CHAPTER SIXTEEN NOTES

1 Antoine Bechara, Daniel Tranel, Antonio Damasio, and Hanna Damasio. "Deciding Advantageously Before Knowing the Advantageous Strategy." *Science 275* (1997): 1293-1295.

2 James Garbarino and Clare Bedard. *Parents under Siege: Why You are the Solution, Not the Problem, in Your Child's Life* (New York, NY: Free Press, 2001).

CHAPTER SEVENTEEN NOTES

1 Pepper Schwartz. *Love Between Equals: How Peer Marriage Really Works.* (New York, NY: Free Press, 1994).

BIBLIOGRAPHY

Aldarondo, Etiony, and Murray Straus. "Screening for Physical Violence in Couple Therapy: Methodological, Practical, and Ethical Considerations." *Family Process* 33 (1994): 425-439.

Bechara, Antoine, Daniel Tranel, Antonio Damasio, and Hanna Damasio. "Deciding Advantageously Before Knowing the Advantageous Strategy." *Science 275* (1997): 1293-1295.

Carlson, Bonnie E., and Louise-Ann McNutt. "Intimate Partner Violence: Intervention in Primary Health Care Settings." In *Battered Women and their Families* edited by Albert R. Roberts, 230-270. New York: Springer, 1998.

Cook, David R., and Anne Franz-Cook. "A Systemic Approach to Wife Battering." *Journal of Marital and Family Therapy* 10 (1984): 83-94.

Erwin, Jonathan C. "Giving Students What They Need." In *Educational Leadership* 61 (2003): 19-23. http://posterous.com/getfile/files.posterous. com/leadingedge/ik5zzohsERHdA5R6rqy2mmI3GZGcM9v9A3F4C8 bFj8o5mtrPEfAnI3DxkFnC/GivngStudntsWhtTheyNd.doc. (accessed March 9, 2011)

Garbarino, James, and Clare Bedard. *Parents under Siege: Why You are the Solution, Not the Problem, in Your Child's Life* (New York, NY: Free Press, 2001).

Geller, Janet A. "Conjoint Therapy for the Treatment of Partner Abuse: Indications and Contraindications." In *Battered Women and Their Families: Intervention Strategies and Treatment Programs,* edited by Albert R. Roberts, 76-96. New York: Springer, 1998.

Gelles, Richard J., and Murray A. Straus. *Intimate Violence.* New York: Simon & Schuster, 1988.

Gottman, John M., Neil S. Jacobson, Regina H. Rushe, Joann Wu Shortt, Julia Babcock, Jaslean J. La Taillade, & Jennifer Waltz. "The Relationship Between Heart Rate Activity, Emotionally Aggressive Behavior and General Violence in Batterers." *Journal of Family Psychology* 9 (1995): 227.

Hart, Barbara J. "The Legal Road to Freedom." In *Battering and Family Therapy: A Feminist Perspective*, edited by Marsali Hansen and Michele Harway, 13-28. Newbury Park, CA: Sage, 1993.

Harway, Michele, and Marsali Hansen. "Therapist Perceptions of Family Violence." In *Battering and Family Therapy: A Feminist Perspective*, edited by Marsali Hansen and Michele Harway, 42-53. Newbury Park, CA: Sage., 1993.

Howatt, Bill. "Discussing the Stress Epidemic in Corporate America." In *Howatt H R Consulting* (2002). http://www.howatthr.com/images/pdf/enhancingdna/Discussing%20the%20Stress%20Epidemic%20in%20Corporate%20America.pdf (accessed March 9, 2011)

Jenkins, Alan. *Invitations to Responsibility: The Therapeutic Engagement of Men who are Violent and Abusive.* Adelaide, South Australia: Dulwich Centre, 1990.

Kirkwood, Catherine. *Leaving Abusive Partners.* London: Sage, 1993.

Larson, Aaron. "Assault and Battery." *Expert Law* (October, 2003), http://www.expertlaw.com/library/personal_injury/assault_battery.html#2 (accessed August 22, 2010).

Leeder, Elaine. *Treating Abuse in Families: A Feminist and Community Approach.* New York: Springer, 1994.

Lees, Sue. "Marital Rape and Marital Murder." In *Home Truths about Domestic Violence: Feminist Influences on Policy and Practice: A*

Bibliography

Reader, edited by Jalna Hanmer and Catherine Itzin, with Sheila Quaid and Debra Wigglesworth, 57-73. New York, NY: Routledge 2000.

Madanes, Chloe. *The Violence of Men: New Techniques for Working with Abusive Families: A Therapy of Social Action.* San Fransciso: Jossey-Bass, 1995.

McHugh, Maureen. "Studying Battered Women and Batterers: Feminist Perspectives on Methodology." In *Battering and Family Therapy: A Feminist Perspective,* edited by Marsali Hansen and Michele Harway, 54-68. Newbury Park, CA: Sage, 1993.

Murphy, Christopher M., and K. Daniel O'Leary. "Psychological Aggression Predicts Physical Aggression in Early Marriage." *Journal of Consulting and Clinical Psychology* 57 (1989): 579-582.

Massey, Mary Anne Banich. "The Neuroscience of Fear." *Family Therapy Magazine* 8 (2009): 22-25.

Osofsky, Howard J., and Joy D. Osofsky. "Violent and Aggressive Behaviors in Youth: A Mental Health and Prevention Perspective." *Psychiatry* 64 (Winter 2001): 285-295.

Polisi, Caroline Johnston. "Spousal Rape Laws Continue to Evolve." *We News* (July 1, 2009), http://www.womensenews.org/story/rape/090701/spousal-rape-laws-continue-evolve (accessed August 22, 2010).

Samuels-Dennis, Joan A., Marilyn Ford-Gilboe, and Susan Ray. "Single Mother's Adverse and Traumatic Experiences and Post-Traumatic Stress Symptoms." *Journal of Family Violence* 26 (2011): 9-20.

Schacht, Rebecca L., Sona Dimidjian, William H. George, and Sara B. Berns. "Domestic Violence Assessment Procedures among Couple Therapists." *Journal of Marital and Family Therapy* 35 (2009): 47-59.

Schlee, Karin Anne, "Wife Abuse: Disentangling the Effects of Psychological and Physical Aggression." *Dissertation Abstracts International: Section B: The Sciences and Engineering* 61 (2000): 549.

Schwartz, Pepper. *Love Between Equals: How Peer Marriage Really Works*. New York, NY: Free Press, 1994.

Siegel, Daniel J. *The Developing Mind: How Relationships and the Brain Interact to Shape Who We Are.* New York: Guilford, 1999.

Sokolova, Irina V. "Depression in Children: What Causes It and How We Can Help." *Medical College of Wisconsin Health News* (December, 2003), http://www.personalityresearch.org/papers/sokolova.html, (accessed April 17, 2005).

Sonkin, Daniel Jay, Del Martin, and Lenore E. Auerbach Walker. *The Male Batterer.* New York: Springer, 1985.

Spertus, Ilyse L., Rachel Yehuda, Cheryl M. Wong, Sarah Halligan, and Stephanie V. Seremetis. "Childhood Emotional Abuse and Neglect as Predictors of Psychological and Physical Symptoms in Women Presenting to a Primary Care Practice." *Child Abuse and Neglect* 27 (2003): 1247-1258.

Steinberg, Marlene, and Maxine Schnall. *The Stranger in the Mirror: Dissociation—the Hidden Epidemic.* New York: Harper-Collins, 2001.

Straus, Murray A. "Leveling, Civility, and Violence in the Family," *Journal of Marriage and the Family* 36 (1974): 13-29.

Straus, Murray, and Robert Gelles. *Physical Violence in American Families: Risk Factors and Adaptations to Violence in 8,145 families.* New Brunswick: Transaction Publishers, 1990.

Straus, Murray, Richard Gelles, and Suzanne K. Steinmetz. *Behind*

Bibliography

Closed Doors: Violence in the American Family. Garden City, NY: Anchor, 1980.

Stritof, Sheri, and Bob Stritof. "Is Marital Rape a Crime?" *About.* http://marriage.about.com/cs/maritalrape/f/maritalrape10.htm (accessed August 22, 2010).

The United States Department of Justice National Survey of Domestic Violence, published in 2000.

2005 WL 3508320, *T.T. v. L. DE J.* CN99-06525, Del. Fam. Ct.

Tyrka, Audrey R., Lawrence H Price, Hung-The Kao, Barbara Porton, Sarah A. Marsella, Linda L. Carpenter. "Childhood Maltreatment and Telomere Shortening: Preliminary Support for an Effect of Early Stress on Cellular Aging." *Biological Psychiatry* 67 (2010): 531-534.

Walker, Lenore. "Legal Self-Defense for Battered Women, in *Battering and Family Therapy: A Feminist Perspective,* edited by Marsali Hansen and Michele Harway, 151-165. Newbury Park, CA: Sage, 1993.

Walker, Lenore E. *The Battered Woman Syndrome.* New York: Springer, 1984.

Ziegelstein, Roy C. "Acute Emotional Stress and Cardiac Arrhythmias." *Journal of the American Medical Association* 298 (2007): 324-329.

About the Author

Dr. Deb Schwarz Hirschhorn holds a PhD in Marriage & Family Therapy from Nova Southeastern University. She is a Licensed Mental Health Counselor, Approved Supervisor and Certified Hypnotherapist in the State of Florida. "Dr Deb" is also licensed in New York, a Clinical Member of the American Association for Marriage & Family Therapy, a Diplomate of the American Psychotherapy Association, a member of MarriageFriendlyTherapists.com and the International Society for Mental Health Online. She has been court-certified as an expert witness in custody cases. She has been in the field 35 years and has taught at universities and has been on radio and TV. She has published in professional journals and has written a hundred articles in newspapers and online.

Please see DrDeb's blog at DrDeb.com and other resources at TheHealingIsMutual.com

CPSIA information can be obtained at www.ICGtesting.com
Printed in the USA
BVOW072258130612

292612BV00001B/1/P